THE ANIM
BROTHERS AND SISTERS

THE ANIMALS ARE OUR BROTHERS AND SISTERS

*Why Animal Experiments are
Misleading and Wrong*

*Responsible Medicine
Based on a Spiritual View of Creation*

WERNER HARTINGER, MD

TEMPLE LODGE

Translated from German by Johanna Collis

The Publishers wish to thank Hildegard Pickles for her love and dedication to the cause of the animals, and for making this published translation possible.

Temple Lodge Publishing
Hillside House, The Square
Forest Row, RH18 5ES

www.templelodge.com

Published by Temple Lodge 2005

Originally published in German under the title *Die Tiere sind unsere Geschwister, Verfehlte Tierversuche und verantworthliche Heilkunde* by Wege Buchhandel und Verlag, Freiburg, in 2002

© Wege Buchhandel und Verlag 2002
This translation © Temple Lodge Publishing 2005

The moral right of the author has been asserted under the Copyright, Designs and Patents Act, 1988

A catalogue record for this book is available from the British Library

ISBN 1 902636 72 4

Cover by Andrew Morgan Design
Typeset by DP Photosetting, Aylesbury, Bucks.
Printed and bound by Cromwell Press Limited, Trowbridge, Wilts.

For my wife Denise

The animals are as much God's children as we are, so they are our brothers and sisters.

St Francis of Assisi

Contents

I am deeply grateful for the support I have received and for many suggestions from friends and those who work to prevent cruelty to animals.

Foreword

Increasingly and in many ways, people today are reconsidering their relationship with the created world, their environment and the cosmos. More and more the varying opinions are coming to centre on whether there is a need for experimentation on animals and what ideas concerning science, medicine and economic criteria result from such experiments.

People's attitude to the animals in their environment is overshadowed by a lack of clarity, various agendas and also their wish to vindicate themselves. Scientific pronouncements, sometimes lacking any serious foundation, and also various expressions from church sources are contributory factors. The atmosphere of enquiry combined with a lack of certainty has persuaded me, as a medical doctor, to summarize our evolutionary links with our fellow creatures from the point of view of spiritual science, on the basis of what Rudolf Steiner had to say about this, and to consider my findings in juxtaposition with present-day thought on medicine and experimentation.

In Steiner's day people's attitude to animals and the environment was not yet so strongly marked by the wish for clarity that exists now, nor had the cruel methods of animal destruction for the supposed good and advantage of humanity reached anything like their present proportions. His remarks on this subject are thus few and far between, scattered among a number of his works. They have been selected and evaluated here in order to highlight the importance of finding creative ways of sharing the earth with all its creatures. I might describe this book as providing clarification on many questions pertaining to human beings and animals with the necessary inclusion of former and current ideas about medicine and other means of healing.

The physical, chemical, biological and physiological laws of nature are the visible and qualifying effects of cosmic laws that reach right into the earthly realm. They could also be termed the laws of creation. The part of this that is recognized and assessed by humans is what we call science. But since science is restricted to substances and processes perceivable by the senses it can only deal with earthbound natural phenomena while lacking the ability to explain them adequately. When science talks of the forces that function less obviously within the physical realm, and therefore remain unrecognized, it describes them as 'supersensible', which always unjustly includes the pejorative hint of being 'unscientific' in the sense of something that cannot be believed. The definition of 'supersensible' can thus only be used justifiably by a science that takes this aspect into account.

In their blinkered ignorance about cosmic aspects, scientists who pursue the materialistic path motivated by egoism and economic factors have brought about a situation of possibly irreversible damage to our planet together with the natural world essential for its survival. Their treatment of our fellow creatures is neither humane nor sensible or morally justifiable, nor does it have anything to do with an attitude of responsibility compatible with creation as a whole.

To counteract the reckless lack of consideration entailed in a technical and economic utilization of scientific knowledge to the detriment of our entire environment it is now a matter of urgency to draw attention to the cosmic sphere and the laws residing in it since these are what form our whole world while also influencing and sustaining our life in it.

We pay remarkably little attention to the basic issues of the laws governing our life. What is their purpose? Where do they come from? Who created them, and why? The psychological importance of such matters and also willingness to understand these things is on the increase, however, so that people are beginning to seek rationally comprehensible and acceptable answers to the questions hitherto sidelined and left unanswered by science. Their intellectual honesty no longer allows them to dismiss our relationship with the cosmos and its supersensible realms as 'unscientific', and indeed a number of 'inexplicable phenomena' have already afforded us glimpses into the significance of those realms.

By enabling us to understand the spiritual background of our existence, spiritual science provides the basis on which natural science can be extended into the supersensible realm. It calls for the same degree of seriousness and effort in its study as any other field of enquiry, and in addition it makes greater demands on our receptivity and ability to think logically where its abstract concepts and their definitions do not have a basis in the perception of what is visible to the senses.

The time has come when spiritual science must no longer remain disqualified and relegated to obscurity as a kind of secret doctrine on the grounds that the knowledge it holds in store about the foundations of our life does not accord with certain vested interests. Spiritual science describes a necessary and correct evolution of all the sciences so that they may reach beyond the boundaries of sense perception and begin to define our place in the cosmos. It is also indispensable as a guide to an understanding of cosmic laws. We must realize that current ways of thinking scientifically are not conducive to expressing or even awakening moral or ethical understanding and feelings such as those needed for an approach to those cosmic laws.

Although on the whole the knowledge revealed by spiritual science calls for a different and more comprehensive way of thinking, it can nevertheless—with some restrictions—be presented in thought forms appropriate for the scientific mentality currently applied to natural phenomena. However, it is neither desirable nor possible to simplify or popularize its content in the type of entertaining or banal packaging people tend to demand nowadays. And indeed serious enquirers or researchers are unlikely to expect such a presentation, for they will be capable of discriminating between objective evaluations and invalid condemnations.

The explanations in this book are addressed not only to readers already interested in spiritual science but also to all those interested in preventing cruelty to animals and protecting the environment. They may gain a firmer basis for and confirmation of their humane views. Medical doctors, researchers and scientists, too, may find here a useful bridge between esoteric and academic knowledge that could lead to the genuine welfare of human beings and the animals and kingdoms of nature entrusted to their care.

Part One

WHY ANIMAL EXPERIMENTS ARE MISLEADING AND WRONG

1

No Cruelty to Animals Means Better Medicine for Humans

In the early days of human life on the earth people did not yet till the soil efficiently or grow produce in a planned way. So the head of a family was obliged to supplement the diet of his dependants by finding food for them among the surrounding animal world. Although he always risked losing his life, being greatly outnumbered by the animals, his chances of success were more or less equal, so he managed to provide what was needed for the relatives in his charge. Before and after a successful hunt he would thank his god for enabling him to return unharmed, and he would also perform rituals to beg forgiveness for invading the sphere of the group spirit of the animal he had killed. Even today such rites are accepted without question among so-called 'primitive' peoples who are entirely familiar with the reasons for them.

Later there came a time among those groups of humanity when certain privileged individuals, owing to the relationship that had developed between them and their 'subordinates', were no longer obliged to support their families by hunting. This led to the beginning of what became hunting for a hobby and the enjoyment of killing without any need. Even today such leisure pursuits remain in our society, although they are now redefined as activities necessary for the protection and nurture of the animal world. They are still engaged in by a relatively small circle of participants. If a competitive attitude of mind had not led to the branding of specific animals whose nature it was to regulate the biotope as 'beasts of prey', hunters would not now be 'obliged' to follow a 'trade' which they evidently rather enjoy!

Another important change in people's attitude towards their fellow creatures came into play in Europe two or three hundred years ago when farmers no longer kept only as much livestock as fitted their land and fulfilled their needs but sought to increase 'yields' by keeping larger herds and purchasing additional fodder.

Only a short time later there then developed the incomprehensible attitude towards achieving even greater profits by means of accelerating the growth and weight gain of stock through administering a variety of pharmacological 'remedies' including hormones to animals that were not sick in the first place. That such weight gain led to a loss of quality and flavour appeared to be of no consequence.

But the limit of exploitation of animals by humans had still not been reached. There appeared on the horizon the supposed possibility of profiting from animals by using them as models for trying out remedies for human illnesses, which of course called for the development of compatible ideas in medicine. It cannot be denied that driven by the profit motive and economic considerations the 'lord of creation' has undergone a steady moral decline in his conduct towards his fellow creatures.

There remains one further important point to consider. While human conduct towards animals in earlier ages was understandable, dictated as it was by circumstances and being insignificant in view of the numbers involved, it was also beneficial to all human beings in some degree. Such a claim cannot be made today either for the mass experiment of large-scale animal husbandry or for the subjection of animals to experimentation for the 'advancement' of medicine. The former has led to a significant deterioration in the quality of meat, including incalculable though constantly disputed detrimental consequences for the consumer, while the latter, through the attitude of mind generated by animal experimentation, has in some instances been catastrophic for the general health of the population.

Many consider themselves to be opponents of cruelty to animals while at the same time failing to take into account the manner in which their own lifestyle as well as their shopping and eating habits and other expectations exploit and take advantage of them.

Opponents of experimentation on animals closely examine the presumed necessity for it in connection with medical knowledge. They recognize the right of animals to live and remain unharmed, and they set themselves up as their defenders.

The cruel destruction of animals through experimentation, however, is morally inadmissible quite independently of any presumed or actual knowledge that might be gained in connection with human diseases, or other advantages. So it is not possible to agree with those opponents of animal experimentation who uncritically accept economic and scientific claims that it is necessary for the furtherance of medicine and merely demand that it be gradually phased out 'in so far as alternative methods can replace it'.

Such an attitude either merely accepts or else ignores all the consequences for humans resulting from animal experimentation in medical research. Such experimentation is given approval if it appears to be profitable or if certain pressure groups back it. Genuine prevention of cruelty to animals, though, is a necessary moral and humane stance in a

Christian society wherever profit is obtained from the torture or unscrupulous exploitation of our fellow creatures.

Opponents of animal experimentation are not only prepared to save animals from suffering a painful death; they also feel obliged unreservedly to draw the attention of others to the consequences of such experimentation. Moral attitudes and ethical thinking must not be allowed to stop where profit begins.

Professor R. Ryder, UK, has pointed out a fundamental contradiction in people's behaviour:

> Scientifically, the experiments are justified by stating that animals and man are similar and comparable while moral justification for the cruel treatment is based on the erroneous supposition that animals feel less pain. Here, too, it will be necessary to decide: Either animal and man differ so greatly that these experiments have no or only minimal usefulness for humans, or the animals are so like us that especially the cruel and fatal experiments are ruled out as a matter of course.*

Animal experimentation cannot and must not be evaluated primarily on the criterion of whether it leads to useful information or not. The key point is that we have no right to cause suffering and death to other living creatures by taking advantage of their innocence or inferiority in order to gain supposed or actual advantages for ourselves.

---

*This originally English quotation has been retranslated from German into English. In some instances Dr Hartinger, now deceased, has stated the name of an author he quotes but not the title of the work. It has not been possible to give full references in these cases nor to locate original English texts.

It is appalling that experimentation on animals, of whatever kind, is taken for granted as being essential for its supposed contribution to the fight against human disease.
Justification is found for any kind of 'contribution', whatever
this may mean, derived from every possible experiment. This
is precisely the attitude that has led to the current excessive
destruction of animal life by experimentation. It is a fatal
mentality founded on the assumption that other living creatures exist merely to be exploited—as were slaves in former
times—for personal advantage and without consideration or
limit.

Nor is this view in any way altered by the existence of
'ethical commissions', which are set up to salve people's
consciences and have the purpose of monitoring experimental
practices and pronouncing them acceptable. Such commissions, of which there are unfortunately many, are the product
of a system that allows for decision-making by majority vote
in bodies that have no real powers to check or decide anything, but merely present a pseudo-legal front which in
addition serves to protect individuals from having to take any
personal or moral responsibility.

On the basis of experience one has to doubt whether
experiments on animals can contribute anything useful for
combating disease in human beings. Hitherto, at any rate,
most such studies have proved ineffective as a guarantee for
the safety and efficacy of medicaments or therapies, or for
providing useful research into the causes of illness that might
lead to suitable and successful treatment. Even after decades
of systematic experimentation on millions of animals the
number of sick people has risen, not fallen; and there are still
no treatments that can tackle the causes of the main illnesses
that are normally fatal. The minimal usefulness of most

animal experiments bares no sensible or justifiable relation to the countless animals sacrificed or the extent of their suffering and death, nor to the huge sums required of taxpayers and patients to finance these efforts. We therefore have to ask how many more of our fellow creatures will have to be annihilated in this way before people begin to realize that conventional, one-sidedly scientific and technical methods of research, diagnosis and therapy can only deal with non-comparable biological laws that differ from species to species and fail to get to grips with the functional totality of a living organism.

We need new and comprehensive models that are oriented towards prevention and include consideration of the physical, psychological and spiritual basis of good health; we need to understand that illnesses are signals by means of which an organism is trying to tell us something important, namely, that something is wrong or inappropriate in our behaviour or lifestyle.

If patients are to be given more than a mere semblance of help we shall have to admit to something that is often side-stepped for opportunistic reasons: it is not possible to remove or, as medical jargon would say, 'eradicate' all hardships, risks or diseases, or pass on the burden of these to others, at the cost of the agony and death of our fellow creatures.

For example the reaction of young animals to radiotherapy and anaesthetics was found to differ from that of older ones. During one 'test' carried out in the evening almost all the laboratory rats died, while during an identical 'test' twelve hours later all survived. In winter the test survival rate may be almost 100 per cent higher than in summer. Mice crowded together in a cage all died after having been treated with a particular substance, whereas those confined in conditions that allowed for their normal social structure all survived. A research group with Professor Grimme at Bremen University, Germany, concluded from the results of their work in 1983: 'The results obtained in animal experiments are valid only in the context of the specific test conditions and not for humans or their illnesses.' *Die Problematik der Wirkungsschwellenwerte in der Pharmakologie und Toxikologie* (Questions of activity thresholds in pharmacology and toxicology).

This conclusion was reached not by opponents of animal experiments but by researchers who had intended to develop a method of testing the effectiveness and results of experiments with animals! The suitability of applying the results of animal experiments to medical research is further disqualified by the fact that the psychosomatic causes and effects in healthy and sick human beings cannot be reproduced or assessed experimentally any more than can the conscious and unconscious spiritual and intellectual control of a person's overall biological makeup.

Medical research at the University of Marburg, Germany, on the human being in the workplace focused on analysing strong biorhythmic fluctuations which showed up not only marked differences in reaction depending on the time of day but also longer fluctuations of up to a year's duration. Specially noticeable were not only the large fluctuations in tolerance of and reaction to medications and chemical substances but also in physical resilience.

On the basis of considerations and observations such as these a great many competent experts and researchers who have applied their critical faculties to assessing the relevance of animal research results to human beings have rejected the usefulness of such research for the human situation. Some have described the relevance of these results to human diseases as pure speculation or, as physiologist Professor Herbert Hensel put it, 'probability theory with even fewer chances of success than a lottery'.

Nevertheless, the general public has for decades been informed by the influential triumvirate of our contemporary age—industry, politics and science—with extensive coverage and cooperation from the media that medical research 'for the benefit of humanity' cannot do without experiments on animals which are needed, so it is said, for testing tolerance to substances as well as for the training of medical doctors. All the achievements of medical science are supposed to have been arrived at or 'found' by means of animal experimentation. Objective and critical refutations of these claims by opponents of animal experimentation, including information about the consequences of such assertions, are frequently quoted in an abbreviated form that invalidates the force of their argument. This occurs despite the fact that pharmacological or other damage resulting from the inappropriate application of results derived from experiments on animals prove that the much vaunted 'benefit to humanity' only reaches a small proportion of the population.

So it is the intention of this book to investigate more thoroughly the arguments put forward in favour of justifying and utilizing the involuntary sacrifices made by our fellow creatures and, as it were, to put all the aspects and consequences under the microscope. Many people emotionally reject the torment of animals and their death through torture without applying their reasoning faculties to it or wishing, or indeed being able, to corroborate the stated scientific usefulness of such actions. Based on experience and objective assessment, numerous scientists have also increasingly turned against animal experimentation even without having gone more deeply into the ethical questions involved. It is evident that despite the torture to death of billions of animals science remains unable clearly and causatively to define the object of its research, namely illness, or to clarify the concept of 'healing'. The assumption is that illness in humans is an accidental disorder of one or several biological processes or chemical/physiological reactions in the body, and that these can be righted by the application of a pharmaceutical substance. This assumption is based on a materialistic attitude of mind that regards the organism as a mechanical interaction of individual functions which may be similarly scrutinized in an 'animal model'. Working with such an assumption and dispensing with a holistic approach to medicine it is logical to resort to animal experimentation and take it for granted that this will throw light on pathological processes and make it possible to develop healing methods. Human diseases are, however, not caused by mechanical processes. The true causes are psychological, so it follows that since they are caused by unwise lifestyles diseases cannot be chemically analysed or physically measured or assessed in accordance with scientific criteria.

With its current methods of research, medical science has adopted the world view of physics. Matter is regarded as the foundation of life processes and the human organism is reduced to the level of a machine. This excludes the essential dimensions of human individuals, namely, the spiritual, psychological and social aspects of their lives. Quite obviously science cannot or does not wish to recognize the real principle of life present in every organism nor to accept the functional variations in the way body, soul and spirit work together even though for a long time now there can hardly have been a single medical discipline in which psychosomatic illnesses have not been increasingly diagnosed and recognized. Illnesses of this kind are of course specific to the individual and can no more be reproduced in animals than can the consequences of years of an unsuitable lifestyle.

During a therapy conference at Freiburg, Germany, in 1987 Professor Gerock stated: 'The majority of people die as the consequence of five diseases which they bring upon themselves through inappropriate diet, lack of exercise, and the consumption of alcohol and nicotine. These are heart disease, hypertension, lung cancer, cirrhosis of the liver and diabetes.'

Since the life expectancy of animals is much lower, and since their psychosomatic reactions cannot be compared with those of humans, and since their tolerance levels and capacities for compensation differ from those of humans, as do their processes of metabolism, detoxification and excretion, how can it be possible to simulate the effects of those various and unnecessary causes of illness in humans and find effective therapies by using animals as models?

In addition, there are clinically similar manifestations of animal and human illnesses for which the causes are rarely identical. And even among individual human beings externally very similar symptoms can have fundamentally different causes, so that any therapeutic interventions will have to be different also. And since the recognizable symptoms of a disease do not necessarily indicate anything significant about the causes even in humans, any comparison between human beings and animals is bound to be speculative. So a transfer of experimental data from the animal experiment to the human situation is quite simply impossible to appraise.

Biologically and medically, the causes of a pathological process in the human being are predominantly to be found in failure of the immune system and the body's capacity for self-healing, neither of which can be likened to damage to the organism that has been artificially induced. In an experiment it is only possible to cause damage in an animal, which amounts to merely reproducing symptoms but not a natural human disease. The previously healthy animal is in an entirely different situation as regards recovery than is a sick human being. In many instances the animal is strong enough to overcome any physical or chemical damage to its body. Yet in too many cases the experimenter attributes this recovery to measures he has taken. He is then surprised when the therapy does not elicit a response in a human patient with an impaired immune system, thus missing the point that for recovery to take place the potential and vitality of the biological organism are decisive rather than the assumed efficacy of a pharmacological substance.

Experiments on animals are furthermore tailored to fit specific research aims and factors, which means that all other causes in the concatenation of a complex reality are extensively obscured and suppressed. The multiplicity of possible triggers, many of which may mutually reinforce one another, are thereby arbitrarily and determinedly reduced to one or only a few factors. This is tantamount to manipulation and does not accord with reality. Since this approach merely leads to a recognition of not very relevant partial truths, there can only be a very one-sided and incomplete view of the illness and how it progresses, and thus also of the possible therapies. Any comprehension of the overall situation or of the risks involved will be lacking.

Another aspect that needs to be taken into account is that animal tolerance of specific substances cannot be compared with that of human beings. Prominent scientists therefore dispute the relevance of animal experimentation to the human situation. Despite having been tested on animals, thousands of medicines have had to be withdrawn from the market owing to serious side-effects unobserved or unsuspected during the tests. It is likely that the true extent in everyday life of the undesirable results or damage caused in this way remains unknown or that in the absence of 'scientific evidence' the causes are not recognized. Expert opinions vouching for risk-free quality would soon disappear if the assessor were to be held personally responsible for his pronouncements and the client for the subsequent manufacture of the product. After all, other citizens also have to stand by what they say and do!

In an article in *Münchener Medizinische Wochenschrift* (34/69) (Munich Medical Weekly Journal) Professor Müller of Munich University's First Gynaecological Hospital described research based on international data on foetal damage caused by medications taken by the mother during pregnancy and their embryo toxicity. According to this research, 90 per cent of malformations in live-born children were caused by 'exogenic factors'. Such factors included medications taken by the mother during pregnancy as well as industrial contacts with specific chemical compounds which may have altered the woman's genetic structure previously in ways that induced malformation in her offspring. According to a study of over 4000 women by Nishimura, the number of stillbirths following medications taken during pregnancy was ten times higher than average.

During the 1976 Internal Medicine Congress at Wiesbaden, Germany, it was stated that about 6 per cent of fatal illnesses and 25 per cent of illnesses requiring hospitalization of the patient were due to the side-effects of medication. A study from Boston, USA, relates that side-effects of medication were observed in about 30 per cent of hospital patients and that 3 per cent of life-threatening conditions resulting from the side-effects of medication required the patient to be hospitalized. At the Berlin-Steglitz Clinic, Germany, the figures given were 20 per cent and 6 per cent respectively.

On the basis of an extensive investigation in 1978, toxicologist Professor Remmer of Tübingen, Germany, calculated that 30,000 fatalities per year in the Federal Republic of Germany resulted from medication and its side or after-effects. This amounted to three times the number of deaths on the road. He concluded his statement with the words: 'The trust people place in medication is incomprehensible; it borders on a belief in miracles. Looked at objectively, the characteristics of medicines and their efficacy offer no justification for such faith!'

Commercial behaviour and pronouncements by scientists have led even medical doctors to lose confidence in the politics of medicine and health. This was shown by a survey of around 1000 specialists in internal medicine conducted by their professional association in the Federal Republic of Germany. Of the participating physicians, 36 per cent disagreed with the advertising produced by the pharmaceutical industry, while a mere 3.6 per cent were satisfied with the information provided by representatives of the industry. Worrying replies were given to the question: 'Are you under the impression that you can trust the statements put out by the pharmaceutical industry?' Only 7.5 per cent answered in the affirmative, while 73.6 per cent trusted the statements only partially. All in all over 80 per cent of the physicians interviewed entertained serious reservations.

The 1979 issue of the medical journal *Diagnosen*

(Diagnoses) reported on the extent to which conventional medical treatments were being applied [in Germany, Tr.]. It was found that 70 per cent of all general practitioners prescribed homoeopathic or natural remedies or other therapies written off by conventional medicine as unscientific 'outsider methods'. Of these, 39 per cent regarded the outsider methods as superior to conventional medicine and a further 37 per cent considered them to be of equal value. Only 4 per cent saw conventional therapies as being better.

Yet the latter enjoy gigantic financial backing. According to statements by the pharmaceutical industry, it spent 2.1 billion Deutschmarks on advertising its products in 1985 alone, while the Federal Association of medical insurance companies spoke of over 5 billion Deutschmarks (2.5 billion Euros).

In medical research, statistics are used increasingly as a basis for evaluating the therapeutic and toxicological effects of chemical substances. The attempt is made to use such summaries of research results as a tool for discovering laws and finding out what causes substances to be effective. This mode of scientific evaluation cannot recognize the causes of illness, however, and is therefore largely meaningless for both doctor and patient since it fails to assess causality.

Surely it is the task of research to discover how and why a medicine helps the patient. The aim should not be to work on the basis of averages but to recognize the pathogenesis and course of each individual case in order to administer a therapy successfully. Only when the real cause of the illness is known and the causal mechanism of how substances work is understood can better therapeutic measures be worked out. Restricting knowledge to a scientific understanding of statistics stands in the way of achieving this insight. Only when all

the basic scientific facts are known do statistics gain a degree
of relevance as supplementary information.

In the fields of surgery and organ transplantation especially, every latest subtlety in the skill of the surgeon is greeted
as an epoch-making breakthrough even though experience
has shown that it will soon be supplanted by the next discovery. Yet the results of research into the prevention of
disease which would render such skills obsolete are scarcely
acknowledged even though they would make much suffering
and the expense of therapies avoidable. Thus less than 1 per
cent of all medical costs is spent on prophylaxis.

Such attitudes take on astonishing forms and dimensions in
connection with the third most fatal disease in humans,
namely, cancer. For years the health authorities have been
granting licences to more than 650 chemical substances used
in food processing to increase the attractiveness of products,
e.g. flavour enhancers, colourings and preservatives used in
the presentation and packaging of foods, and also in cosmetics. And many other substances are used in agricultural
production including animal husbandry right along the entire
chain from producer to consumer. Many of these substances
are carcinogenic.

This means that with their food the population are con-
suming chemical products, pharmaceutical substances and
pesticide residues harmful to their health in unknowable
quantities throughout their lives! It is recognized without
contradiction that the majority of all cancers in humans are
triggered by environmental influences such as the consumption or application of chemicals in foods, general lifestyle or
other external uses or influences. Yet in the interest of the
profit motive the industry presents uninformed consumers,
without asking them whether they want this, with 1500

substances, some of them toxic and carcinogenic, that are used and remain in the food they eat or are intended for daily external or internal use whence they then enter the environment and its cycle of life. All these substances are licensed by health authorities for use in the interests of commercial gain and they have all been declared 'safe' on the basis of tests on animals.

In order to treat 'successfully' the cancers that have been caused in humans chiefly in this way, billions of animals have for decades been tortured to death, the purpose of this inappropriate objective being to discover further chemical substances with which to treat the illnesses already caused by similar ones. There is no doubt that the production of this huge variety and amount of chemicals is commercially profitable, that the food production linked to it is profitable, that diseases in humans and animals are profitable, that researching and treating these diseases is profitable and that, last but not least, the manufacture of medicines with which to treat them is profitable. Should consumers be willing to put up with the risk of having cancer for this reason?

I shall conclude this chapter with a few words on the moral aspect of vivisection. Representatives of the established churches have been wonderfully united in repeated 'official' statements on this theme, presenting as a part of Christian thinking the supposed 'right' of human beings to 'use and exploit' their fellow creatures for purposes which serve their own ends. On the other hand there is little consideration of the resulting cruelty to animals, of the paucity of usefulness to humans, of the frequently unnecessary duplication of experiments, or of the consequent risks for the consumer. Justification for these questionable attitudes tends to be based on biblical texts which are given arbitrary interpretations that do not fit in with the Christian ethic and lack any recognition of the truth as a foundation for our moral attitudes. Indeed, their comprehension calls for an unacceptable degree of mental acrobatics.

Regrettably, industry employs similar criteria for judging its self-chosen task, thus influencing science and research in its favour, pointing them in a direction which similarly regards moral attitudes as unjustified hindrances obstructing their right to experiment on animals. In view of this situation there is an urgent need for critical self-examination with regard to this type of research and style of exploitation, and indeed in connection with the whole of our relationship with our fellow creatures. Since scientific attitudes are so stuck in a rut, and since good health is to such a large degree regarded as a commodity that has to be adapted to the wishes and unrealistic demands of the wider population, it will be difficult to draw attention once again to the real causes of human diseases. Help will be required if this is to be achieved.

In the nineteenth century, medical research was set on the path of animal experimentation by Claude Bernard with the motto: 'Why think if you can experiment!' It is now high time, not only in the interests of the animals themselves, to replace this attitude founded on animal experimentation and the renunciation of thinking with one involving thinking and the renunciation of animal experimentation. Experiments are not suitable for obtaining knowledge about human diseases or the fundamentals of healing, for it is in these very processes that animals and humans differ profoundly. So animals cannot provide us with any usable or permanent information that might be relevant for our physical or psychological health.

There are three different reasons that motivate us both to

reject animal experimentation conducted in the course of searching for medical treatments beneficial to human beings and also to work for the cessation of such experimentation.

1. *Factual aspects.* Owing to the differences that exist between human beings and animals—the wide variations in reactions, effects and tolerance of chemical substances, and the total incomparability of acceptable toxicity levels and the effects of pharmaceutical medications including their metabolic breakdown—no sufficiently acceptable results relevant to human consumption can be obtained. In addition, degrees of tolerance, allergies, side-effects and the effect of combining various substances cannot be comparably reproduced or assessed on the basis of animal experiments. Likewise, the psychosomatic causes of human diseases cannot be simulated or evaluated in animals, and thus no knowledge about their pathogenesis or possible therapies can be gleaned.

2. *Medical aspects.* The scale of animal experimentation in research, diagnostics and therapy of human diseases has fixed medical work at a mechanistic, materialistic level, so that it is no longer able to rise to more far-reaching insights into the causes of disease, the nature of the healing process, the psychosomatic and spiritual functioning of biological organisms and their reactions, or their dependence on terrestrial and cosmic forces.

3. *Ethical and moral aspects.* From this point of view experiments on animals are untenable not only on account of the suffering they cause to the animals but also because they place heavy psychological burdens on wide swathes of the population, leading to associated tendencies to ill health.

All historical concepts of morality, all ethical persuasions arising from religious sources and passed down to us unchanged, and also the esoteric statements of Christianity forbid the killing of our fellow creatures by means of cruelty and torture even if it leads to some serviceable results. Any teachings on this subject forbid such actions and characterize them as inhumane and immoral. These actions do not become morally justifiable merely because they might bring benefit to us or because they are necessary for the advancement of science. Every unprejudiced individual will recognize the injustice of such actions.

2
Questionable Experiments and Laws

For various reasons some would prefer the following remarks and trains of thought not to reach all ears. However, as a wise man said a long time ago: 'He who desires to find the source is obliged to swim against the current.' It is gratifying and a proof of its quality if a saying can still be applied correctly and meaningfully after thousands of years.

Remaining in antiquity for a moment, we might add that more than two thousand years ago one of Plato's pupils was asked why he persisted in putting forward his unusual ideas in public even though they found acceptance only among a small minority. The reply is said to have been: 'Even if only a single drop of the thoughts is taken up, the ocean of human wisdom will be augmented!' How modest one was in those times!

Although intending no offence, one cannot help asking whether it is not highly unlikely that the reasons put forward by the scientific community to justify animal experimentation in research, industry and medicine will still be known even one hundred years from now. Possibly they will, but then merely as examples recorded in medical history.

For as long as Germany's federal government has been in existence there can hardly have been a bill more controversial or more opposed by wide sections of the population than the proposed law for the protection of animals. This may be taken as a welcome sign of the urgent need to rethink the relationship between human affairs and, especially, the animal world. Owing to outdated assumptions, there is much that is out of kilter here and will need revising in the way we view and regulate such things if we are to move from a mentality of exploitation to one of fellow feeling with creation. In medicine such a change of attitude touches on fundamental concepts relating to the cause and treatment of diseases in human beings.

Essential thinking based on humanitarian ideas has always initially been upheld only by a small band of those who understood and supported it, and those few have usually met with stern opposition from the direction of established interests.

Current extensive experimentation on animals in research and medicine must be critically assessed from three aspects:

1. Can the knowledge and data about animals gained from these experiments be applied to human situations? If so, to what extent? What kind of assurances are possible and what are the risks?
2. It is claimed that it is possible to simulate human diseases on the animal model, to acquire a new understanding of the causes of these diseases, and develop therapies as a result. Is this claim correct in principle and relevant to such statements?
3. In view of the acknowledged moral concepts of our culture, are we at all justified in inflicting suffering and pain on countless animals and killing them under torment for any presumed or actual advantage to ourselves?

Faced with the enormous advertising budgets available to industry and science with their numerous organizations for extensive and expensive publicity campaigns in which they present their ideas, and faced with the one-sided stance of politicians whose attitude to commercial interests on the one hand and those of the consumer on the other is not even-handed, and faced with the correspondingly biased media, those who want to prevent cruelty to animals can only offer their unselfish and unpaid efforts on behalf of their fellow creatures, combined with a view of animal experimentation that is not partisan but critical of such experimentation on objective and ethical grounds.

It is impossible to arrive at a common denominator for this complex situation. Attitudes towards the need and justification for animal experimentation range from ethical though scientifically insufficiently comprehended dislike of inflicting pain on animals at one end of the scale to the researcher's goal-oriented motivation which takes no account of such sensibilities at the opposite end. The compelling impression is that the industry regards animal experimentation as a means to achieving optimum profits while politicians see in it an opportunity to evade the responsibility which they claim to exercise.

A further astonishing and revealing criterion put forward as a justification for animal experimentation is the claim made by researchers with remarkable self-assurance that such experimentation automatically becomes acceptable if a scientist so much as glimpses some medical problem or other!

The deplorable ploy of harping on people's fear that if animal experimentation were to be given up people would fall ill and die through lack of suitable treatments, however, is no longer quite as convincing as it once was. That is why the trumped up claim is now in circulation that if animal experimentation were to cease research would fall behind, workplaces would be lost and scientists would go abroad—despite the fact that within the overall framework of scientific research animal experiments only account for an insignificant amount. They could be abandoned in favour of other human related research leading to better medical insights without any fear of losing workplaces since alternative research would require an equivalent number of workplaces.

Despite competent opinions from specialists in their own departments, it is estimated that the experimental consumption of animals in research, industry and medicine worldwide amounts to 300 million annually, which is to say that more than one million animals are more or less slowly tortured to death per working day.

No one can justify this as a necessity; and even less can it be reconciled with any meaningful coordination of research projects. Equally there can be no talk of an 'indispensable quantity'. This exorbitant number of victims alone points up the scale of unmonitored, parallel and competing work on experimental objectives, duplicated many times over in various establishments. This of itself gives rise to considerable doubts as to the claimed 'necessity' of the experiments.

Such unimaginable destruction of animal life is allowed within the law because of inappropriate legislation and surveillance and is made possible by an uncoordinated licensing system. It is promoted by politicians and carried out, because of the varying interests of industry and research, with the help of countless unsympathetic and pitiless helpers and dealers and is silently tolerated and co-financed by a large, ill-informed body of consumers. The experiments are pursued for purposes of research, carried out to satisfy licensing regulations, and justified as being required for the purpose of establishing toxicity limits (LD50 test) and assessing tolerance levels (Draize test). All this is done despite the fact that surely science, industry and the legislative bodies are perfectly aware of the fact that experimentation on animals cannot yield any useful information either about the efficacy or toxicity or about adequate safety limits in respect of chemical and pharmaceutical substances intended for human consumption.

Animal experiments also yield less than adequate information about how foreign substances behave in the human body and whether they cause side-effects, allergies or damage when consumed in combination with foods or medications. They are equally useless in ascertaining tolerance levels of foreign chemical substances or their metabolic breakdown in respect of medicine for humans.

The assessment of toxicity limits such as the no-effect level or the acceptable daily intake does not include any consideration of the fact that experimental cell damage sets in morphologically, microbiologically and physiologically long before any observable symptoms of illness appear, or that regardless of non-assessable tolerance differences the damaging or therapeutic effect sets in very variably in the animal or the human patient and, while remaining clinically undetectable, begins to take effect as soon as the zero line is crossed.

All tests with control groups show that the fear, pain and stress of the laboratory animal, combined with its isolation in an unfamiliar environment, lead to unforeseeable changes that cannot be evaluated either before or afterwards. This was confirmed yet again by the work at Bremen University *Die Problematik der Wirkungsschwellenwerte in der Pharmakologie und Toxikologie* (see p. 13).

This reports that owing to unquantifiable external and internal influences, tolerance levels and reactions in the animals varied so widely that it was impossible to arrive at a generally valid assessment of the effects of chemical substances. The conclusion reached was that the test results could not be evaluated in accordance with clinical and scientific criteria and that furthermore any application to the human situation was impossible.

Criticism of such a conclusion must be backed up by a clearly defined moral attitude. To ignore this when reaching a decision or taking action is tantamount to hiding a light under a bushel, perhaps the most important light in the make-up of the human being, namely, the light of moral understanding.

It is therefore not right to accuse animal research opponents of being emotional and consequently lacking in scientific objectivity. Their indignation at the treatment meted out to our fellow creatures is entirely justified, arising as it does from their moral stance.

We should also not forget that there are fundamental differences between the arguments put forward by those in favour of animal experimentation and those who are against it in that the latter have no professional or commercial axe to grind in the way they see things. Indeed, their efforts on behalf of the animals entail expense and trouble, take up their free time and lead to their being vilified. They take all this upon themselves and base their fellow-feeling with the creatures of this world not on fears of illness but on recommendations that lead to health.

As a justification for animal experiments it is repeatedly claimed that one therapy or diagnostic method or another which has proved medically useful for the treatment of humans was only arrived at or 'found' thanks to experimentation on animals. Seen superficially, this claim to have dispatched billions of animals to their death by torture appears credible, indeed even impressive.

Any detailed discussion of the matter can, however, only lead to one conclusion, namely, that the administration of a specific dose of a specific substance in a specific circumstance led to a specific reaction or function change in the animal, or that a specific intervention was well or badly tolerated by the animal's organism. Any interpretation beyond this for the purpose of applying it to the human situation can at best be a hypothesis of unquantifiable value and not a scientifically founded statement relevant to the medical treatment of human beings.

Many researchers in all disciplines continue to point out that experiments on animals cannot yield any information on effects, efficacy or tolerance in respect of the human organism. They therefore understand the necessity for conducting the same tests on humans and indeed resolutely call for such verification.

'Toxicological tests on animals which are supposed to support the risk-free application of a substance to humans merely serve to provide an alibi.' Dr Kienle, Dr Burghardt and Dr Knipping in *Fortschritte der Medizin* (Progress in medicine), 12/87.

'Animal experimentation with a view to ascertaining the effectiveness of medication for humans is a nonsense!' Professor Hardegg, Conference on Laboratory Animals, Hanover 1972.

Animal experimentation does not allow us to conclude that the human organism will react in the same way. There are substances that show more than a thousandfold difference between their effectiveness and tolerance levels in animals or man. Others produce reactions that are entirely different or even the opposite. If in addition the metabolic breakdown, the detoxification and excretory mechanisms are in large measure incomparable, if the bio-mechanical compatibility and the ability to react or compensate provide insufficient evidence of compatibility with the human organism, if allergies, side-effects, long-term damage and the effects of combinations with other chemical substances taken in from food or other medications cannot be reproduced on an 'animal model', then the extrapolation of animal experimentation onto the human situation presents an incalculable risk.

These findings cannot be altered by the frequently mentioned transferability quotas that are always put forward as the measure of the usefulness of animal experiments and often greatly exaggerated. Such quotas can only be calculated when similar and comparable experiments done on humans can be put forward. Until this becomes possible, such data are not available nor can they be calculated. But once they do become available as 'clinically proven' through human experimentation, they immediately become uninteresting and unnecessary because the results thus obtained will anyway make for better and less risky medicine for human beings. Only in this way, and not by means of using animals, can knowledge about the reactions of and effects on the human organism be discovered.

Many millions of animals have been painfully tortured to death or had LD50 experiments carried out on them in the search for methods by which data obtained from them might be transferred to humans. One team of researchers—who were not opposed to animal experimentation—reached the following conclusion after carrying out such experiments: 'Tolerance levels obtained by animal experimentation are valid solely with reference to the experiment in question. They apply only to effect A when procedure B is used on laboratory animal C at time D when the result is obtained by method E.

The data are thus unique and cannot even be applied to other animals!' *Die Problematik der Wirkungsschwellenwerte in der Pharmakologie und Toxikologie* (see p. 13).

In contrast to what is often asserted, the relatively risk-free use and dosages of substances and also the methods and surgical techniques discovered experimentally for the treatment of humans are not based on animal experiments. Professor M. Beddow Bayly of the British Royal College of Surgeons stated in this connection: 'No discovery in medicine exists that can be traced back to experimentation on animals ... Medical research using animals must be condemned on the basis of three accusations: because of its cruelty, because of its uselessness for humans, and because it hinders genuine progress in medical science!'

If usable knowledge on the effect, dosage and tolerance of substances can only be obtained by tests on human beings, then surely any preceding tests on animals cannot be described as necessary for medical science! After accepting criticism along these lines, a good number of scientists experimenting on animals have been known to cease such work on behalf of medical science and have had the inner stature to go public about the erroneous assumption that such research yields any usable or justifiable data. In *Victims of Science*, Professor Ryder of Oxford University stated: 'I do not believe that the suffering I have caused to animals in experiments—a good many, alas—has been in the least helpful to humanity.'

We might add the words of Dr Kienle (and colleagues): 'Experiments on animals are meaningless and an illusion, and cannot be applied to human beings.' *Analyse einer Illusion* (Analysis of an illusion).

And Professor Pickering of Cambridge University has

written: 'The opinion is frequently heard that fundamental truths may be revealed by animal experiments and may then be transferred to sick human beings. As an experienced physiologist I feel justified in taking a stand on this: It is pure nonsense!' (*British Medical Journal*, 64).

There is also no need or justification for the experiments carried out by lecturers at their own discretion as demonstrations used in training medical students and personnel. What educational purpose is served by students having to kill frogs in order to test their nervous reaction? What is the point of allowing countless dogs to bleed to death every semester in order to demonstrate what happens when the circulatory system fails, or of showing the beating heart in a dog's opened-up chest cavity in order to demonstrate what happens when it stops or how medical, physical and manual manipulation can be applied to restart it?

Neither the anatomy of an animal's chest cavity nor the external circumstances can be even remotely compared to what is needed to restart a human heart that has stopped beating. It is from work carried out in an accident and emergency department or an intensive care ward that valuable knowledge can be gleaned. According to the law as it stands now there should already be an obligation to desist from experimentation on animals if the same teaching purpose can be fulfilled by technological facilities such as films, projections, models and so on.

Many student protests at universities against the torture and killing of animals, and also legal wrangles, confirm that such teaching methods are unnecessary and serve no educational purpose.

The need for the training of surgeons to be based on animal experimentation is also frequently brought up. The claim here is that practice on animals is needed for the development of manual surgical skills and experience. This claim, too, cannot be accepted without objection.

Training leading to qualification as a surgeon begins with acquiring basic knowledge through observing the work of a teaching surgeon in general surgery or accident departments. Then the trainee is gradually allowed to gather experience and skills under the eye of his teacher who then finally decides when he is ready to begin working independently. Special skills in microsurgery and other operative specialities are learned in the same way and do not presuppose any need for experimentation.

The purpose of practising on a living 'animal model' is to learn how to adapt one's manual skill to different situations as seen by the eye. The fact that most rats and rabbits are usually killed immediately after the practice session only goes to show that there was never any intention of observing a process of recovery and that the outcome of the operation was irrelevant. The methods in question have long since become routine in surgery and all the worthwhile techniques are practised in almost every hospital.

The need for surgical training on live animals is usually put down to shortage of time, insufficient manual practice or inadequate operating experience. Generally in the USA and Anglo-Saxon countries such supplementary practice is carried out on vascular models or on vessels with different sizes of lumen in animal or human placentas.

A similar point can be made with regard to transplant surgery. The problem is not the operative skills, which the surgeon already has. Trouble arises in the post-operative period when there is a degree of intolerance to the transplanted organ so that the patient's body tries to reject it. This risk cannot, however, be tested on animal models which can also not yield any information concerning the effect, dosage and tolerance of the required immune suppressives in the human being.

In experimental surgery, too, the animal's different physiology, tolerance and ability to compensate makes it impossible to extrapolate the outcome of postoperative recovery—with or without complications—to the human situation.

For example, an articulation model, including the combination of materials to be used, the statics involved and the best production method, can be optimally designed by computer in the laboratory. This also applies to assessment of its durability, strength and other physical properties. All this can be done much better in this way than by experimenting on animals, and this also goes for ascertaining human tolerance and tissue reactions, which cannot be done sufficiently accurately by using animals.

Professor Luigi Sprovieri spoke for many surgeons and surgical disciplines. He was one of the inventors of extracorporeal blood circulation and a colleague of the heart transplant pioneer Dubost at the University of Paris. Speaking in Sorrento in 1980 before hundreds of his colleagues from many countries he said: 'Biomedical research does not need animals. It is useless and also dangerous to continue with these traditional methods. The difference between humans and animals is too great and therefore usually misleading. We are increasingly finding that artificial organs can be used in human beings without first being tested on animals. Artificial heart valves and also pacemakers were first tested on humans.'

In a similar vein, it is not essential to use animals for

teamwork training in the operating theatre. Thousands of surgeons, orthopaedic surgeons, ear specialists and others, including their teams, have become competent and responsible operators without ever having to practise on animals.

Professor Larson Tait, UK, emphasized: 'I reject the idea that operating on animals is necessary for training purposes. Such procedures ought to be unconditionally prohibited!'

And we might add the following remarks by Professor Desjardin, President of the French Society of Surgeons in Paris: 'Having learned about surgical techniques and the overcoming of difficulties by observation, one can then begin to operate oneself under supervision. This is the real way in which surgeons are trained, and I maintain without reservation that there is no other method! A skilled surgeon can learn nothing from experimenting on animals, and a beginner only learns the wrong techniques. I have never met a good surgeon who had learned anything through experimenting on animals!'

The daily 'consumption' of test animals of all sizes is estimated to amount to one million. Precise figures are unobtainable because there is no available official registration system. The greater part of the experiments is legal, so requires no special permission but only notification.

Other experiments [in Germany, Tr.] require permission from various regional police or local authorities, but there is no coordination of information. Such coordination is equally lacking in respect of the many computerized registers of the work being done.

The immense number of experiments can never be classed by anyone as being 'necessary', let alone justified in any way. Still less do they represent an 'indispensable number' which interested parties claim to require and which the initiators of the animal protection law have legalized. This sanctioned destruction of animals carried out simultaneously in many establishments shows that similar experiments are being undertaken without supervision for reasons of competition, which in itself negates the claim that there is a need and makes a nonsense of there being an 'indispensable number'.

On the basis of legislation, ethical commissions with memberships that do not represent an equal spread of views are able to set the number, type, duration and dimension of experiments while also using the supposedly democratic set-up to cover themselves both personally and morally against accusations of irresponsibility. In addition to non-existent registration of projects and their outcome, other reasons for the excessive number of animals used are the lack of any requirement to prove knowledge of previous experimentation results, failure to publish important research results and the practice of granting permission without imposing any obligation to submit results for assessment.

It has yet again become necessary to withdraw many hundreds of medicines from the market because they have caused severe toxicological, organic and tissue damage and also genetic damage in humans, none of which showed up in prior experiments on animals because the incomparability of tolerance levels and of detoxification and excretory processes made this impossible. Over many years an enormous rise in allergic skin and organ diseases has been observed. These give rise to virtually insurmountable medical and also social problems. These consequences, too, cannot be brought to light through animal experiments because they are species specific.

At the 1977 Congress on Internal Medicine at Karlsruhe, Germany, it was stated that 6 per cent of all fatal diseases and about 25 per cent of diseases in general were attributable to damage caused by medication. At the subsequent congress in 1987 Professor Gerock stated that half of all fatal diseases could be prevented by adherence to an appropriate lifestyle.

In cases of fatality caused by medication the laconic statement is often heard that this cannot be helped since no therapy is without risk. Apart from the fact that this is not true, it also confirms what opponents of animal experimentation repeatedly maintain, which is that guarantees of safety in medication cannot be based on such experiments.

Even the legislature considers that the transfer of animal experiment results to humans poses an incalculable and unacceptable risk. Therefore, in addition to tests on animals already undertaken, it calls for there to be comprehensive clinical tests proving efficacy, harmlessness and tolerability before any medicine or diagnostic or therapeutic method is brought onto the market.

So, contrary to what is claimed, the relatively risk-free use of medicines as well as diagnostic and therapeutic measures does not depend on animal testing at all, but on the tests on humans conducted before registration is granted. Statements based on experimentation on animals to the effect that results obtained cannot be applied to humans therefore only go to show that the requirements of medical treatment of human beings cannot have been the reason for 'working with the' animal model'.

Even the most copious users of research animals occasionally put their cards openly on the table. Professor J. D. Gallagher, Medical Director of the firm of Lederle, for example, said in 1964: 'Animal experimentation is carried out for legal and not for scientific reasons. In many cases it is pointless to ascribe future value to these studies.' And Dr

Weidmann, Pharmacological Director of the firm of Sandoz, was of the opinion in 1982: 'Toxic reactions of the human immune system cannot be demonstrated on the animal model.'

3
Meaningless Test Results

Everyone is inclined to assume that legislation for the good of the population will reflect all the scientific evidence and research results available. In most cases, however, the transposition of scientific knowledge into legislation is based on criteria that are inappropriate to the subject matter but are chosen to comply with various vested interests, the result being that scientific truth frequently gets lost somewhere along the way. Such are the circumstances that hold sway in the making of laws and regulations that are supposed to protect our fellow citizens' health. In order to increase rather than abandon the commercial utilization of chemical products, the inappropriate assumption is made that below specific concentrations and accumulations in the organism such chemicals have no injurious effects.

In keeping with these criteria, in 1974 the Advisory Council on the Environment set very stringent no effect levels for every substance, which would ensure no damage to the organism even when consumed regularly for life. In addition the acceptable daily intake was worked out for which a safety factor was included in the calculation. The scientific reasoning behind this attempt to establish supposed tolerance and toxicity levels rests on the arbitrary assumption that cells contain substance-specific receptors and that a corresponding dose-effect correlation exists.

However, it should also be mentioned that none of the relevant literature contains any generally valid definition of the concepts 'effect' and 'non-effect'. Nor do the best known scientists and specialist authors accept the claim that there is such a thing as a dose of a foreign substance so small that it would not have any effect on a biological organism. Almost all of them consider that every chemical substance introduced into an organism will initially bring about a functional alteration even if this is clinically undetectable and cannot be proven by physical-chemical means. There is no such thing as a dose so small that it does not have any effect. Even after decades experimenting on animals, Professor Zbinden wrote in 1979 that a 'no effect level' does not exist.

Since on the one hand there is no generally valid definition of the concepts 'effect' and 'non-effect' and since on the other hand further uncertainties are added by the insoluble problem of differing sensitivities in biological systems, it is impossible to reach an objective evaluation, so that only subjective criteria remain as the basis for any decision.

In addition there exist numerous different receptor theories none of which covers the whole range of phenomena and effects brought about by the introduction of a pharmaco-logical substance into an organism. These various theories, on which the calculation of toxicity levels is largely based, thus provide no valid evidence regarding the totality of effects and are therefore inadequate as far as meeting the stated requirements is concerned.

Factors insufficiently catered for in this calculation are above all the inappropriate supposition that the action of the active principle is dose-dependent, and in addition the cir-cumstance that in the human being there are other substance effects in addition to the one being investigated. So the basis for the calculation does not accord in any way with the actual pressure to which the organ is being subjected. This is because the human organism is exposed not only to a single chemical substance but also to an unquantifiable variety of external effects both below and above the postulated activity thresholds.

In this system of calculating toxicity there are also further factors about which specialist circles are not in agreement. The incorrect assumption is made that the effect a substance has on a biological organism depends solely on the size of the dose and the duration of the influence. Account is not taken of the fact that the reaction depends to a great extent on the degree of immunity and the health of the biological system rather than on the quality or quantity of the noxious substance.

There are considerable differences between humans and animals in respect of tolerance and effect. The risk involved in claiming assumed similarities cannot be reduced by claiming that the most sensitive and comparable animal species are to be used and that a transfer quotient has been calculated. This is a cover-up because the choice of the number of animals of the species to be used and of the most sensitive tests to be done presupposes knowledge about the intended effect in humans, yet the transfer quotient can only be calculated once the results of tests on human beings are available. Before these are available the tests can neither be assessed nor calculated. In order to select the most suitable animal species, the effect profile in the human being must be known. Yet if the effect profile is indeed already known, then animal experiments are no longer needed since the data obtained by tests on humans are much more accurate and appropriate than those based on the calculated transfer of an incalculable and variable experimental figure.

Therefore, for the 'protection of consumers', toxicity calculations include a so-called 'safety factor' as an attempt to compensate for the range of variations in the way biological organisms react. But even the Advisory Council was unable to work out generally acceptable scientific criteria for its findings, so that in every country and establishment the 'safety factor' is an arbitrary figure lying somewhere between 0 and 100.

In their ground-breaking work already mentioned (p. 13), *Die Problematik der Wirkungsschwellenwerte in der Pharmakologie und Toxikologie*, Professor Grimme and his colleagues thus concluded in 1983:

> Pharmacological data and toxicity thresholds are intended to register the biological effects of substances and quantify their toxicity. On account of biological variability, however, it is not possible to establish fixed magnitudes, because such thresholds vary from individual to individual and from point in time to point in time, as well as a variety of genetic and environmental parameters and interactions of unknown proportions. This makes statements of 'standard figures' questionable, lends a further dimension to data from animal experimentation, and has removed the basis on which the traditional view of medicinal effectiveness being measurable in specific doses was founded.
>
> Biological variability makes it impossible to define activity thresholds in relation to no effect levels. It also makes it impossible to define reliable activity levels for specific toxicological effects, e.g. risk, transferability and tolerance. The lack of a firm foundation on which such calculations are made thus becomes evident, and this then conceals the lack of knowledge about the phenomenon of biological effects and reactions. In view of the many uncertainties in assessing the biological effects of harmful

substances and the lack of knowledge about how they will behave, maximum dose specifications cannot carry out the intended task of protecting the health of human beings and the environment. A typical example of how the lack of knowledge is trivialized and disguised may be seen in the formulation always brought forward by authorities, politicians and industry in cases where maximum doses have been exceeded: 'There was at no time any danger to the population.' What ought to be said is: 'The population is endangered at all times by the lack of a proper basis for calculations, by the uncertainties involved, by the impossibility of calculating the results of transference and by the alleged scientific basis of data.'

In spite of all this, for the sake of the commercial though otherwise non-urgent use of countless chemical substances, a toxicity calculation has been constructed and dressed up as being scientifically based and intended as a protection for the consumer. The basic data include either suppositions, refutable theories or untenable 'facts'. Meanwhile the following real facts are ignored:

1. There is no such thing as an activity threshold below which an amount of a chemical substance introduced into an organism has no effect. There is also no clear line between a dose so low that it is not effective and one slightly higher that is.

2. As a part of the calculation, the receptor theory is an attempt at interpretation which does not allow for adequate explanations for all the effect phenomena. The existence of several, in some cases mutually exclusive, theories shows up the inadequacies of the assessment basis over against biological functioning.

3. The assumption of a correlation between dose and effect based on amount and time as the sole factors in changes occurring is untenable. There is a failure to realize that an effect depends mainly on the affected organism's stamina and ability to compensate.

4. The 'no effect level' and 'acceptable daily intake' thresholds are based on commercial considerations; they are unscientific and disguise the real biological facts.

5. The mode of calculating supposed tolerance levels of chemical substances does not take into account that as a result of the above attitude, people are not confronted with one substance in isolation but with countless chemical combinations of which neither the quality and quantity nor the combined effect have been even approximately grasped.

6. The basic data on which the calculations are based relate to animal experimentation results and leave out of account not only the fact that humans and animals differ in their tolerance and ability to compensate but also the fact that the way their metabolic systems break down and excrete foreign substances, often involving the creation of toxic intermediate products, means that they cannot be compared.

7. The safety factor, incorporated into the calculations because of these biological variations, is not founded on any science-based experience but rather on sometimes even contradictory assessment criteria. It is nowhere adequately defined nor is there an obligation to hold to it. It is fixed to accord with interests not related to the scientific content; it is arbitrarily varied and is frequently changed.

These ideas call for considerable mental acrobatics when they are applied to probably the most serious realm of human disease. All scientific disciplines recognize that 80 to 90 per cent of cancers in humans are triggered by chemical substances entering the body via food, medication, cosmetics, clothing or environmental conditions. The obvious conclusion to draw from this would be that to protect consumers the use of chemicals should be at least drastically reduced but certainly not increased. Well over one thousand chemicals are used in the planting, manufacture and processing of food products up to the point of sale. They enter the human organism in an uncontrolled way, and when used on animals are known to be carcinogenic. As is the case with formaldehyde, perchloroethane and many others, their use and thus their forced consumption is, however, permitted, the given reason being that the results of animal experimentation cannot be transferred to humans. Yet the basic connection between foreign chemical substances and cancer is not in doubt. People's anxiety is dispelled by the 'no effect' levels and 'acceptable daily intake' levels of consumption which are supposed to make the substances non-toxic and tolerable. These, however, are worked out on the basis of the inadequate methods of calculation arising from animal experimentation and ignore the very fact that it is impossible to monitor the amounts of the substances absorbed.

And this is not all. Enormous subsidies and grants have been received for decades by countless establishments for research to find further chemical combinations by means of which the frequently fatal illnesses already caused can be treated and exterminated. One cannot help asking what further explanations and opinions the population can be expected to accept from scientists and politicians.

More can also be said about the toxicity evaluations arrived at through animal experimentation. Every necessary experiment is carried out using the loathsome LD50 test to which in America alone 5 to 6 million animals fall victim. Although it would be possible and certainly financially expedient to do so, in many instances results obtained in other countries are not taken into account, so that the same tests in similar orders of magnitude are carried out in other national establishments and thus unnecessarily repeated for the sake of form. These experiments submit our fellow creatures without anaesthetic to terrible suffering, fear and pain leading to cruel deaths (dosages increased until half of the animals die). Yet the results of these experiments are utterly meaningless for humans and can provide no information about the important long-term effects. That is why many scientists refuse to undertake them. Their evaluation ranges from meaningless via deceptive to beastly. Even hardened experts describe them as ritualized mass extermination of animals.

When we consider the regular fluctuation of LD50 test results, the small degree of usefulness they have for humans and also the circumstance that they are then used as a basis for the more than problematical method of calculating hypothetical activity thresholds which serve only the purpose of hiding the dangers and constructing legality for the commercial utilization of chemical substances, we cannot help finding that this throws a peculiar light on those who are in favour of such experiments.

For decades world-wide, uncoordinated, competing and for the most part unmonitored research costing unimaginable amounts of money and incalculable numbers of animal lives has been ongoing into the 'causes' of cancer in the human being. It is hard to use the word 'research' for this, for research is understood to mean an unprejudiced investigative activity that takes account of all aspects.

Despite this surely unique expenditure of money, animals and investment, very little is known about how malignant tumours arise in human beings. With variations from country to country, cancer has meanwhile risen to one of the foremost causes of death from fatal illness. No successful therapy has yet been worked out. As was the situation when research began about 70 years ago, we still have to depend on mutilating methods of surgery, radiation and chemistry without being able to exercise much influence over the fatal outcome.

It is possible to cause cancerous growths in animals by using chemical or physical irritation, transplantation or injecting tumour tissue. But these cannot be compared with the spontaneous growth of such tumours in humans; nor can they be cured. In addition to other important biochemical and morphological differences, experimentally generated carcinomas do not develop downright metastasization which is, after all, what causes the fatal outcome of the disease in humans. In apes, the animals most closely related to us, malignant tumours cannot be caused by comparable chemical or physical means.

Although well-documented cures often do occur without any of the classical therapies, there is almost always a reluctance among academic researchers to embark on a systematic investigation of such 'paramedical' successes. Indeed, some astonishing reasons are put forward for ignoring these results. Considering what is certainly unsatisfactory progress from the patients' point of view and considering the many competent statements that exist about the uselessness of research using animals, surely every possible therapy ought to receive unreserved scrutiny.

Together with animal experiments to determine the causes of cancer in humans, the use of animals in searching for anticancer drugs is also globally one of the most disputed fields of biomedical experimental practice. After more than 60 years of research using billions of fatally tortured animals it has still only been possible to develop an effective treatment, though not a cure, for a few fast-growing types of cancer on the basis of a cytostatic which, however, can have serious or even fatal side-effects. The cancers in question are lymphatic leukaemia in children, acute myeloid leukaemia in adults, lymphogranulomatosis, ovarian cancer, small-cell bronchogenic carcinoma, Wilm's tumour in children, and testicular neoplasms in young men. These however, only account for a small proportion of all cancer cases. No successful therapy has as yet been found for any of the others.

Two internationally recognized cancer researchers may be quoted here.

In 1978, Professor H. Oeser stated: 'Researchers in the field of cancer always maintain that conclusions about how cancer arises in humans can be drawn from the results of experiments on animals. As an oncologist with a good deal of experience behind me I cannot agree with this. When you take into account the enormous amounts of carcinogenic substances that have to be fed to, injected into or implanted in the test animals before a tumour actually appears it becomes obvious that this has been caused by poisoning.'

And in 1985, Professor Bruce, director of a university in California, wrote in a report: 'Tests on animals provide no evidence about the carcinogenic effects of chemical substances. Risk calculations based on such tests are hypothetical. Observations on humans are the only reliable source of information. Since there is controversy even about the varying reactions of rodents—the most-used test species—any resulting conclusions drawn with reference to the higher mammals or even humans can only be regarded as pure speculation.'

We frequently hear or read about a cure for the fatal blood disease leukaemia involving the recently developed method of bone marrow transplantation, and this success is quoted as a justification for animal experimentation. However, one cannot assess the chances of a cure without knowing which of the many varieties of the disease is meant, which forms can be successfully treated by marrow transplantation, and what the conditions are. There are over 20 known varieties of leukaemia.

The objective fact is that a relatively successful cure for leukaemia by means of marrow transplantation has only been achieved for acute lymphatic leukaemia and then only in childhood. This type of leukaemia, however, also shows the best reactions to medical treatment, and this is usually the preferred treatment today. Transplantation requires the suppression of the patient's immune defences for a considerable period of time, and this can obviously be more damaging than the treatment itself, since it can result in severe or even fatal infections and subsequent illnesses.

As far as the knowledge said to have been gained about transplantation through animal experiments is concerned, we must remind ourselves that in medicine an 'invention' has never been made in the way this is possible in the technological field. In its empirical nature, medical science, which might be termed an 'experiential art', does not lend itself to this mode of discovery.

Further knowledge gained always builds on the experience of earlier scientists. This is copiously passed on to students and physicians during the course of their training and is further documented in medical publications. When all this is added to an individual's own knowledge and experience it can lead to further diagnostic and therapeutic steps being taken. What are sometimes termed 'inventions' are nothing of the sort, since they all build on the knowledge and experience of previous work and are unthinkable without it.

Far be it from me to want to belittle or detract from any achievements. However, seen from this angle bone marrow transplantation as a therapy for acute lymphatic leukaemia is not even much of a further development of existing knowledge, since it has been a known and used therapy method for a long time. In fact in accident surgery it has been in use for more than 80 years, and still today to transplant marrow and spongiosa in various forms is the method of choice in bone substance trauma.

In a similar way, decades ago therapy attempts for various leukaemias were made using (sometimes several and repeated) blood transfusions and also various methods of infusion or application of sternal aspirate and spongiosa aspirate. Therefore from the point of view either of surgery or of internal medicine marrow transplantation cannot be regarded as a new discovery.

We should mention that animals do not contract a disease that can be likened to leukaemia in human beings. Thus tolerance and therapeutic effectiveness of transplants in animal experiments cannot be evaluated in relation to humans. In fact this must be said of all organ transplantation.

Finally, I would like to stress that the above statements are not in any way intended to be polemical. They seemed appropriate as a way of expressing appreciation of the work of older colleagues and are intended to state facts as they really are and also prevent the raising of unrealistic hopes.

4
Animal Experiments Are Not Necessary

At the end of 1984 the John Hopkins University in Baltimore, USA, hosted an international scientific symposium on alternative methods of diagnosis and therapy in medicine. For many years the unimaginable cost of animal experiments in relation to the unsatisfactory and barely usable results has been reason enough for Americans to take a closer look at this type of research. It was sad to note that of 200 researchers and establishments present only two came from German-speaking countries despite claims that alternative research is constantly on the increase in these countries.

In his opening address Professor Goldberg, director of the research centre at the John Hopkins University, expressly noted that regrettably neither Austria nor the German Federal Republic nor Switzerland were home to systematic efforts to search for alternatives to animal experimentation. He pointed to a lack of collaboration with the universities in those countries.

Representatives of alternative research are of the opinion that it is possible to reduce animal experimentation despite pressure from commercial and scientific interests. From the purely scientific point of view preconditions for this do exist. However, it is feared that scientific considerations alone will not provide the decisive impetus for the form and dimension of future experimental concepts.

This possible reduction would not even cover 50 per cent of all experiments on animals that test toxicity, tolerability, carcinogenicity, teratogenicity (causing malformations), mutagenicity and other aspects. They are also not applicable in the almost equal number of experiments in the research and clinical fields because they cannot replicate the function and reactions of an organism and the degree to which these can be influenced.

Although the outcome of this type of research is not sufficiently successful, the medical world and the general public continue to demand better medicines for more and more different and new types of illness because they regard such medicines as the only possible form of treatment as they are not keen on the possibly inconvenient or commercially uninteresting idea of prophylaxis. The pharmaceutical industry will be the driving force in this general wish for pills to suit every disease without any need to make lifestyle changes, since this is its foundation and what it thrives on.

We shall have to reckon with a steady increase of animal experimentation backed by both science and legislation so long as there is acceptance and legal support for the claim that medicines can be tested on animals in the effort to discover what causes disease in humans, where toxicity thresholds lie and how tolerance levels can be calculated with reference to the human organism.

Even alternative researchers do not, on the whole, question the usefulness of animal experimentation in connection with medical research, nor do they object to it on humanitarian grounds. They have the same personal, professional and commercial interest in its abolition as do the experimenters in its continuation. This indicates that possible clashes of opinion between those who are for and those who are against experimenting on animals are not about the scientific suitability of the experiments or their moral justification, but, it seems, only about concern regarding the share of the medical research 'market'.

The alternative methods that have been developed, which yield data that are far more meaningful and usable than experiments on animals, could already replace almost all required research now done on animals for the purpose of establishing toxicity and tolerance. Yet under the pretext of the need to validate them the introduction of such methods has been blocked for years, even though many other tests that have been in use for a long time, such as the LD50 test, have never been validated. They will only be used in the pharmaceutical industry if they gain the same legal dispensations in civil law as are at present enjoyed by animal experimentation methods. This has not been the case so far, and there is little interest in alternative methods among researchers.

It is not unusual for an opponent of animal experimentation to be asked reproachfully whether he will refuse to have his children vaccinated or not take medicines when he is ill, since all these have of course been 'developed and tested' by means of experiments on animals. Such questions only go to show that the questioner has not informed himself adequately about the arguments in favour of opposing animal experiments in medical research.

From birth, every animal carries in its various organs both bacteria and, above all, viruses which do not make the host animal ill. These are not necessarily destroyed completely in vaccine production, and when they and their toxins then cross the species barrier together with the vaccination serum they cause diseases in the recipient organism. It is known that they can lead to cancer tumours, various other tumours, leukaemias and also other late damage. Professor Clausen of Odensa University, USA, said in 1974: 'Many millions of people have been treated with polio vaccinations that contained the carcinogenic virus SV-40 which is present in monkey kidneys.'

Detailed statistical studies by the German Federal Ministry of Health have shown that all the usual and recommended vaccinations for children and adults do not at present show any influence on the epidemiological graphs for infectious diseases that might point to a reduction of infections. In fact, a clear reduction in the diseases was provable long before the relevant vaccination programmes were set up.

On the basis of world-wide observations over many years the World Health Organization has ended compulsory smallpox vaccination, and this has been implemented here in Germany. Consideration of the advantages and disadvantages of this vaccination had led to this recommendation because in spite of tourism, international trade and unvaccinated immigrants there had been no deaths from smallpox for decades, whereas by causing inflammation of the meninges the vaccination serum had caused permanent damage including mental and physical disorders and even death in some cases.

Similar consequences have been observed more or less frequently in connection with nearly all the usual vaccinations. This raises the question as to whether doctors and parents are morally justified in risking the use of vaccination against illnesses that are not seriously dangerous and have only a low rate of infection when such vaccinations can lead to a known number of healthy children becoming mentally and physically disabled and needing a lifetime of care.

The following considerations will quickly show why it is beside the point to reproach someone for acting 'illogically' if they prescribe or take medications 'tested on animals':

1. The circumstance that experiments have been and are being made on animals does not prove they are necessary or usable in relation to making medicines for humans. Nor does it prove that similar or even better results could not have been obtained by other means.

2. When doctors prescribe or patients take allopathic medicines, this does not mean that they agree with the experimental 'testing' of such medicines on animals or consider such tests meaningful or useful. Since the hypothetical results of the tests on animals are always subsequently 'clinically tested' on people, the relatively risk-free use of such medicines does not stem from the animal tests but from the results of the extensive testing on humans prior to licensing.

3. Moreover, opponents of experiments on animals are not against medical research, as is often said of them. Based on experience, however, they are justified in their view that the required knowledge about human diseases cannot be gained from animals and that quite apart from any supposed or actual advantages it might have, this cruel form of our egotistic exploitation of our fellow creatures cannot be justified.

Medical science founded on animal experiments approaches the matter from the idea that illnesses in humans are for the most part undeserved happenings inflicted on the individual by fate and caused by one or several biological processes and chemo-physiological reactions of the organism. It regards the body as an ensemble of separate parts and functions which, in the way they are presumed to exist in the human being, can be simulated by means of animal 'models' with the purpose of arriving at therapies suitable for humans.

The consequences of this concept and of neglecting to undertake any prophylactic measures are not only a constant increase in chronic diseases but also serious or even fatal side-effects of medicaments which, after cruel testing on millions of animals, are pronounced innocuous and harmless for humans. Despite these masses of animal victims humanity has not grown any healthier. In fact, in America, the country engaging in the most excessive experimental destruction of animals 'for the benefit of humanity', the average life-span is among the lowest of all western countries. What else can be expected when most of those affected suffer from illnesses that they themselves have brought about by wrong or unsuitable nutrition, lack of exercise, and the consumption of alcohol and nicotine, while the others are afflicted by psychosomatic disorders?

Neither the one nor the other of these types of disease caused by civilization can be tested on animals. Animals have a much lower life expectancy and their psychosomatic reactions cannot be compared with those of humans; they have different tolerance levels and their processes of metabolism, detoxification and excretion also differ. It is also unlikely that such diseases can be treated successfully with a chemical substance.

The socio-political aspect is also important enough to be considered briefly here. An 'animal protection law' can and must be based solely on moral principles, as is the case for all laws. When industry, vivisectors, politicians, mass livestock holders who call themselves farmers, animal traders and others who profit from animal husbandry and exploitation reach a compromise agreement on the legally permitted and commercially motivated torture and killing of our fellow creatures, this does no justice at all to those moral principles, and the result cannot lay any claim to the description of 'animal protection law'.

A 'politically enforceable resolution' of such important and fundamental questions in a civilized state at this level is compatible neither with the criteria on which assessments are made nor with general concepts of morality or ethical sensibilities, nor with ideas that are everywhere considered to be true.

It is shocking to see animal experiments so easily taken for granted on the grounds that they are supposed to be indispensable for medical research in that they are said to contribute to combating diseases in humans. Apart from the fact that the conclusion as to their usefulness and indispensability is reached by the very people who are interested in conducting the experiments, this attitude also assumes that any imaginable experiment can and may be deemed justifiable. The legal formulation does indeed permit this provided that a relevant explanation is given. But this attitude is based on the fatal mental attitude according to which unmitigated use may be made of animals as if they were disposable commodities—just like slaves in the past. If the population were even only partially informed about the burden imposed on animals right up to their violent deaths, surely public opposition to such treatment of our fellow creatures would be of quite a different order.

The point is not, of course, whether the vivisector can square his actions with his conscience, but whether his actions conform to general ideas of morality. If every action that a person can square with his own conscience were also automatically full of integrity, then every action that breaks the law would also have to be excused.

Many centuries before the time of Christ, and like a

precursor of what later became the Christian ethic, compassion for our fellow creatures was preached and people were exhorted to exercise responsibility towards other living beings and respect their right to life and safety. This religious attitude is still advocated by many millions and says quite unequivocally: 'It is better to suffer oneself than to cause suffering in others.'

No religious idea passed down to us in its original form, including Christianity, and no philosophy or other definition of morality has ever regarded as permissible the torment or torture to death of animals. In every cultural age, unless it had grown decadent, such behaviour was deemed immoral and therefore forbidden.

An immoral action does not become morally acceptable through being justified as serving one's own requirements or classified as 'scientifically necessary'. And the number of reasons for rejecting experiments on animals can only grow when we remember: that they also fail to yield any sufficiently usable or transferable knowledge for diagnosis and therapy of illnesses in human beings, thus making verification of their results by tests on humans indispensable; that such experiments are carried out for commercial reasons; and that their use in medicine has led and is likely to lead in some instances to considerable damage being done.

There are passages in the Bible which one often hears wrongly interpreted in ways that do not accord with the truly Christian ethic. Thus Pope John Paul II expressed the view that man is justified in exploiting his fellow creatures for his own use. In contrast, his predecessor, Pope Pius XII, formulated his view on this subject in the Vatican Manifesto of 10 November 1950: 'The animal kingdom, like the whole of creation, reveals to us God's power, wisdom and goodness.

Human beings therefore owe it respect and protection. Every thoughtless killing of animals, every cruelty and unnecessary mistreatment contradicts any healthy human sentiment. The role of the animal kingdom within the plan of creation does not consist in being the object of exploitation of whatever kind!'

During the inauguration ceremony of the Medical Academy at the University of Delhi, Mahatma Gandhi expressed himself even more clearly on this important subject: 'Vivisection is the blackest of all the black crimes of which humanity is guilty against God and his creation!'

Another criterion on which to base one's judgement is Lev Kopelev's statement that 'the most shameful cruelty towards our fellow creatures is the one that boasts with seeming modesty of having served the state, the law or some other exalted abstraction'.

Faced with these unequivocal moral definitions of our relationship with our fellow creatures and the environment, how can anyone regard vivisection or other experimental work on animals—whatever the circumstances or reasons— as permissible or compatible with his conscience?

In view of what he saw as the human being's superiority in intellect and knowledge, Friedrich Nietzsche rightly also considered humanity to have a greater degree of responsibility towards the animal kingdom: 'People constantly maintain that animals have no intelligence or moral feelings. Do they believe that our behaviour towards our fellow creatures can be described as intelligent or moral?'

We might add, with Professor Max Thürkauf of Basle, Switzerland: 'The point is not to condemn science as devilish but to show where the devil in science lies. Where experts fail is in their boundless overestimation; without any personal liability they guarantee certainty by calculating the incalculable unpredictabilities of life...'

5
The Responsibility of the Medical Profession

It is estimated that world-wide for years 300 million animals have been tortured and killed annually in experiments carried out in the name of science for the benefit of human health. Both the legislature in the person of the politicians responsible and the experimenters themselves consider that they are not only justified in this because it enables them to gain insights relevant to human diseases, but also that this is an appropriate and morally responsible activity.

Just as the numerical scale of this experimental destruction of animals is impossible to imagine, so is the suffering and mortal fear suffered by those tortured creatures that is caused day after day—evidently without any sympathy—by scientists and their helpers for the presumed benefit of humanity or for the sake of some medical theory that is supposed to lead to cures for sick people.

Although very many of our contemporaries reject such questionably useful and supposedly essential experiments simply on the grounds that they cause so much pain and anxiety to the animals, those involved and those responsible remain as unimpressed by this as by the fact that many, often catastrophic, side-effects are caused in humans by substances and medicaments tested on animals. So they see no reason to attempt a critical appraisal of research on animals for the purpose of obtaining data to be applied to humans. The experimenters are, however, hypersensitive in the way they counter the perceptions put forward by opponents of animal experimentation who disagree with treating animals as disposable commodities. One cannot help noticing that the ethical motivation behind the protesters' attitude is neither considered nor respected and also that the countless expert publications pointing out the inadequacies of animal experiments in respect of human diseases and therapies are ignored.

When scientists acting as expert witnesses in court cases state that the results of experiments on animals cannot be applied to human situations, whereupon the courts rule that the drug manufacturers cannot be held responsible for their use, double standards then appear when those same expert witnesses in their role as scientists go on to maintain that medicine needs experiments on animals, whereupon these are given credence and legalized by the legislature in the interests of safety for users and patients.

Many psychologists and psychiatrists have sought to outline the motivations of vivisectors in numerous discussions and papers in order to ascertain their reasoning and thus possibly justify such actions. They all agree on the professional intentions involved; but, in examining psychological motivations, depth psychology has oscillated between pointing to lack of emotions, difficulties in forming relationships and lack of empathy, as well as to necrophilia in various combinations; sadism and perversion were also named alongside other emotional anomalies, and confirmed in detail. More detailed psychological opinions may be found in works by G. Ciaburri, H. Stiller, F. W. Doucet, A. Plack, E. F. Sievers and E. Fromm, to name only a few.

In his book *Vivisektion* (1937), G. Ciaburri reports on the following incident which has also been documented in an impressive painting. During an experimental physiology course a beautiful dog was brought to the professor. When the animal was placed on the marble slab and noticed the knife and other instruments of torture it sensed this signalled an agonizing death. The poor creature began to howl in fear and lifted its paw as if pleading for mercy, turning its tear-filled eyes up to its tormentor. But it was all in vain and a waste of time. Much moved, the students begged the professor to sell them the animal for whatever price, but to no avail. For several days the dog was subjected to the cruellest tortures and repeated experiments until, on the third day after the depicted scene, it did indeed die in agonizing pain.

Such experiments, of which the general public were increasingly becoming aware, caused the well-known psychologist, theologian and philosopher Ude, from Graz, Austria, to conclude: 'The vivisector is either a morally weak human being with psychopathic tendencies or, if he is of a normal disposition, an utter criminal!'

Perhaps these words were spoken out of the moral theologian's understandable indignation. Nevertheless, an analysis of the circumstances and manifestations does not provide an explanation for changes in character involving a lack of any kind of compassion. In spite of economic, professional or other advantages to be gained from such experiments, even if committed in desperation, most people would feel them to be blatantly wrong and would therefore refrain from committing them not only out of compassion but also on these grounds.

For those with the relevant knowledge one would also wish to add as a further element of understanding that we should remember the religious experiences of times gone by and also the fact that influences going against creation or described as being anti-Christian are defined as 'influences of black magic'. In ritualistic circles of this kind part of the 'basic training' includes the candidate having to stab and cut the

flesh of a living animal with a knife and increasingly trans-
form the torment and pain thus induced into feelings of
pleasurable lust in himself. Frequently such motivations are
the reason for horrible cruelty to animals in all realms of daily
life which in most cases remain unexplained and are in general
classified as sadism.

We can all now understand what Mahatma Gandhi meant
when he said: 'Vivisection is the blackest of all the black
crimes of which humanity is guilty against God and his
creation!' The great esoteric teacher Rudolf Steiner was most
uniquely qualified to investigate such influences. He stated
that nothing was more potent than killing as a means of
acquiring such destructive powers.

During the course of extensive investigations H. Stiller
asked many experimenters about the reasons for wanting to
work in their rather unusual field without there being any real
necessity for it. The majority of those questioned were
unanimous in their reply: 'Because I enjoy experimenting on
animals!'

There was a professor in Hamburg who had spent years
mutilating cats in his experiments. He displayed his attitude
to his professional work on a banner visible throughout his
laboratory which read: 'The main thing is: Work is fun!'

How is it thinkable that a physician can lack any sympathy
or compassion for a living creature and misuse its unsus-
pecting trust when these attributes ought to have been the
very reason for his choice of profession? How can such
actions be reconciled with the Hippocratic oath that obliges
the physician to protect and maintain life?

In former times the physician's profession was the one that
drew most strongly on a person's humanity. People recognized that only an independent individual in society could

develop his own values and moral criteria in which there would be no contradiction between the ethical and the scientific aspects.

Today, however, when physicians finish their university education they find themselves in an unenviable position. Their studies have provided them with quantities of medical and scientific concepts and ideas about which they are as yet unable to form their own opinion. They have been given a conception of medicine and a way of thinking that has been almost doctrinally predisposed towards industry, one that regards as gospel truth anything that is based on a higher authority, although who has declared this authority to be one evidently remains irrelevant.

Their training has not brought them into contact with earlier modes of acquiring medical knowledge, nor has it taught them anything about the personal relationship as a healing influence on the sick organism, or about natural methods of healing, phytotherapy or psychosomatic methods.

Laws now dictate that physicians may only apply 'scientifically recognized' methods of healing. Medical insurance companies [in Germany, Tr.] do not pay for the costs of other methods. Legislation also means that these physicians can be held financially responsible if they fail to follow the rules. And, not least, the recognized healing methods are determined and backed by the very physicians who have developed them on the basis of their own academic training; furthermore, the selfsame scientists may also be called as expert witnesses by courts of law.

So the intuitive path of determining and treating disease, which is the foundation of a genuine art of healing, has been abandoned in favour of a purely scientific, organ-based medicine involving tests on animals; the world view of the physicist has been adopted, one that regards matter as the origin of life. This ignores the most essential dimensions of the individual human being, the spiritual, psychological and social dimensions, and the human organism is reduced to the level of something like a machine.

Nothing much is left today of an overreaching art of healing or the knowledge concerning the non-physical forces also present in an organism. Hippocrates (c. 460 BC) passed on to us comprehensive reports based on medical knowledge still valid today concerning epidemics, febrile conditions, epilepsy and bone fractures. He distinguished between benign and malignant tumours and repeatedly pointed to the importance of hygiene for the patient and the ethical qualification of the doctor. Complicated surgical interventions such as intestinal sutures, lithotomy, nose operations, tracheotomy, trepanning, removal of gall and kidney stones, major brain surgery and thoracotomy in cases of suppurating pleurisy were also known in his day. Apart from various psychosomatic therapies, the only treatments Hippocrates used were herbal. He summarized his knowledge in the well-known saying: 'Nature is the best healer.'

Dr Salivas, Paris, the famous medical historian, expressed the following opinion: 'The immortal Hippocrates never experimented on animals, yet he raised the physician's art to heights from which we are far removed today despite all the great medical discoveries.'

The example he followed was that of Asclepius who had lived about 400 years earlier and who had practised his healing art in a similar way. Greek legend tells us that in his youth his father, the god Apollo, had sent him into the mountains where he spent some time as a pupil of the centaur

Chiron who taught him about the healing powers of the cosmos, the plants and the earth. The concept of 'going into the mountains' is the ancient mystical term for undergoing a special kind of training.

Asclepius established hospitals where he put his patients into a therapeutic slumber in order then to engage with their souls, influencing them and healing them while making contact with their demons which were the causes of their illnesses. He never ceased to point out the connection between negative ways of thinking, faulty lifestyles and disease. In his opinion it was the task of the physician to increase the natural powers of healing and to guide the patient, while at all costs desisting from using therapeutic methods that would add to the load already borne by the body.

A precondition for such knowledge of medicine and therapy last practised by Paracelsus is that those who wish to heal must first purify and develop their own thoughts and thus their own being. They must develop qualities within themselves and absorb knowledge that will enable them to perceive the life processes within an organism and in their relation to the environment, and also the organism's structure and the influences that are making it ill.

When by suitable schooling, self-discipline and experience they have first of all acquired the concepts and then the insights into healing methods that work psychosomatically and into the human being's dependence on the cosmos, and have then gained a new and different conception of the nature of illness in the human being and how it is healed, then they will realize: Only the knowledge one has first developed within oneself can work in a healing way, and all the healing that takes place between one person and another rests solely on this.

The cognitive background to the therapeutic knowledge of that time was the empirical and intuitive concept and understanding that both the human and the animal organism is ruled by a species-specific superior guiding principle that is responsible for the healing process and underlies the overall ongoing flow of life.

People in those days also knew that the visible signs of disease were merely the end product of a pathological process in the soul that had remained unnoticed for a long time and was actually the expression of the fact that the self-healing principle of the organism had been overtaxed. Such realizations combined with the relevant therapeutic methods now come to the fore in homoeopathy, natural healing methods, holistic medicine, anthroposophically extended medicine and psychosomatic medicine.

Our orthodox medical science, on the other hand, has been unable to rise either to a recognition or to an unprejudiced examination of this knowledge; it accepts a psychosomatic connection only where it is impossible to deny such a link, while declaring itself unwilling to see this principle as underlying other illnesses, let alone the process of healing.

In Britain, as we know, questions of spiritual knowledge are approached with a greater degree of objectivity. The existence of a superior, non-material 'organizational principle' is presumed to exist in every living creature, determining its physical shape and preserving the species, and research is carried on into this at a number of universities and the larger research establishments.

There is greater open-mindedness in France, too, evidently owing to that country's long-standing links with overseas cultures. A few years ago the Faculté de Médecine de Paris conducted research into the healing methods and knowledge about diseases prevalent in those cultures. Similar basic knowledge is also confirmed in J. Fontaine's book *La méde-cine des trois corps*. This author mentioned that he was only able to organize and clarify the broader ideas he had gained once he had read Rudolf Steiner's book *How to Know Higher Worlds*.

The knowledge to be found in the writings of the physicians of antiquity, in the various religious persuasions and in eso-teric and anthroposophical bodies of thought could never have led to the idea that it might be necessary to practise vivisection. Physicians with knowledge of that kind would have rejected any idea of torturing or killing another living creature either for personal advantage or to comply with an egoistic way of thinking prevailing in groups. Apart from understanding that no medical knowledge relevant for humans could be gained by such practices, they would also have known that the psychological emotions of animals are quite different from those of human beings in their form, origins and dimensions. Animals experience joy with their whole body and show it in the way they express it, and they experience pain not only at the point where it is being inflicted. The whole animal is seized by the pain, and because it lacks the intellectual capacity to understand what is going on this pain is also magnified into an unbearable fear of death which no one realizing this would have been prepared to inflict.

Such people would also have known that vivisection arises from a materialistic rather than a spiritual way of thinking which lacks any knowledge of the kind possessed by a true physician and which sees the body as an arbitrary mechanical interplay of separate parts, functions and reactions.

This latter attitude is the only logical one on which

experimentation on animals can be based since it presupposes in animals an interplay that is the same as the one in humans, thus enabling pathological processes and cures to be discovered. Some concepts obtained by this means might indeed be correct, but the explanations and reasoning concerning the processes involved and the methods of how they are applied are as unsuitable and useless as are the corresponding therapeutic measures.

Only those who neither know nor want to know anything about the real life-principle of an organism or about the functional interplay between spirit, soul and body and their mutual interdependence and individual specificity can embark on vivisection. Such people are for the most part entirely unaware of the various consequences for themselves and their environment. Long ago the medical schools and Mystery centres of the ancient world knew about the links between the life of an individual creature and the life principle of the cosmos as a whole. They were aware that there is a causal link between taking away life or inflicting pain on a living creature and the cosmos itself to the effect that such actions diminish the noblest powers of human nature, so that torturing or killing another living creature changes something in the person, making him incapable of influencing his fellow human beings in a beneficial or healing way.

The logical conclusion to be drawn from these ideas is of course that we should undertake a far-reaching reappraisal of our thinking leading to the transition from allopathic to natural remedies, homoeopathy and psychosomatic medicine while moving the emphasis of medicine from therapy to prophylaxis by changing our lifestyle and diet and also by bringing about a fundamental transformation of the criteria according to which we choose medicine as a profession, train doctors and see their position in society.

Such a transformation in our general and medical view of the world which would involve considerable, not only financial, changes is, of course, not at all in line with the ideas of established science, research and industry. This is probably one of the main reasons why there is such resistance to abolishing experimentation on animals, for such experimentation exercises a legal and thus 'valuable' function as an alibi. The difficulty of facing such processes of re-thinking which human evolution often makes necessary, involving the transformation of opinions held by established powers, and especially the conflict under discussion here between medicine, ethics and science, was already obvious to Goethe: 'A fallacious doctrine can scarcely be refuted because it is based upon the conviction that something false is true.'

There is much in contemporary medical science and professional training that is based on a lack of freedom in thinking and also a lack of medical 'intuition'. Physicians who are striving for understanding and embark on a path of discovery that is not egoistic can become aware of spiritual laws that imbue the world, that expand their knowledge and fill them with deeply religious feelings which would benefit their healing skills.

The widely known physician Dr Schlegel who worked in Tübingen, Germany, around the turn of the twentieth century may be seen as a symptomatic example of those who sought for ways out of the conflicts and contradictions that really ought not to exist at all between being a doctor, practising healing, medical matters and science. Having made a lifelong study of every past and present medical idea, he persisted in recommending to his patients that they eat a natural diet and practise healthy ways of thinking just as Hippocrates had recommended more than 2000 years ago.

For thousands of years there was no conflict between the science and the ethics of medicine; in fact they were mutually complementary. Science, moral understanding, the knowledge of healing and experience of medicine joined together in the physician for the benefit of the sick, for in olden times the physician was a priest with medical skills and much esoteric and cosmic wisdom. All traditional medical knowledge about our close links with nature, the spiritual wisdom regarding the human being and his dependence on the cosmos and also about the real causes of diseases and how they arise and about how healing works—all this harks back to those 'priest-physicians'.

Today's scientific, social and medical habits of thinking need to undergo a radical reversal with the aim of bringing morality back into the thoughts and feelings of science, and of improving how people relate one to another, to their environment and especially to the animal world to which we owe an evolutionary debt.

We need to regain knowledge about the differing psychological and spiritual structures of living creatures and develop clear conceptual and scientific definitions about what life is, about sickness and healing, about sleep and death. Such knowledge is essential for all medical and scientific research, diagnosis and therapy. Only when the medical sciences have once more acquired this lost knowledge and begun to teach it to their young doctors, only when they begin to accept religious, philosophical and ethical ideas as the foundation upon which they work, will they be able to develop ways of healing the human soul and body. Then the physician will be what he should be and what he was in the past: an unselfish friend and helper for his patients who, thanks to the knowledge he has himself acquired and although he himself might be imperfect as a human being, will be able to re-establish the respect due to his profession and its significance for society and its influence on cultural developments which it once enjoyed in days long gone.

People would then also come to realize that the Hippocratic oath brings with it the obligation to preserve every life and that experiments on animals cannot possibly yield information about the causes of disease in humans but instead inflict on us all the final grim consequences of such activities. There would then be an end to the constant increase of the heavy burden now resting on humanity as the result of the agony, suffering, fear and death of billions of our fellow creatures that have been tortured to death. The great poet Christian Morgenstern expressed his thoughts about this as follows: 'Aeons of love will be needed to pay off humanity's debt to the animals!'

And finally here is something Martin Luther had to say on this subject: 'You will become the best researchers and philosophers of nature when you learn to regard living creatures as a part of creation that is waiting in anticipation, sighing and aching, loathing that which is and yearning for that which will be in the future and which therefore is not yet.'

6
Christian Teachings Concerning Animals

Those of us who are not involved find it difficult to comprehend how all our Churches join forces not only in observing and tolerating the present profit-oriented exploitation and harrowing killing of our fellow creatures regardless of all implications, while otherwise holding fundamentally differing views on many other issues, but also in claiming that such actions are in harmony with statements in the Bible, whereby they even seek to back them with interpretations of Gospel texts.

According to repeated statements by leading clerics from the two main denominations, it is justifiable for humans to make use of animals to their advantage, to profit from their existence and even to kill them when this serves the purpose in hand, while the 'How', the 'How many' and the 'Why' are evidently irrelevant.

Many explanations describe this situation as the divinely bestowed 'right' of the 'lord of creation'. According to a report in *Osservatore Romano* of 24 October 1982, Pope John Paul II stated before, among others, an international delegation of biologists at the Vatican's Academy of Sciences: 'It is definitely the case that animals were created to be of service to humanity, so it is permissible for them to be used also for experimental purposes.'

This statement legitimizing the profitable and also cruel 'use' of our fellow creatures, including their death and beyond, is frequently given emphasis by quotations from the Gospels. People appear to have no qualms in attempting the quite considerable mental acrobatics required in order to see any connection at all between the passages cited and the justification they are supposed to provide. Nor does it seem to matter that such justifications contradict all our moral standards and cannot be felt or qualified as being either Christian or indeed legal.

The many individuals from their own circles appear to have been forgotten who, like Francis of Assisi, exhorted Christians in the past to be true to creation in the way they treated its creatures and repeatedly pointed to our evolutionary duty towards the animal kingdom as an essential foundation for Christian life and work.

Also forgotten are more recent comments by Pope Pius XII on animal experimentation and intensive animal husbandry as a profitable large-scale experiment utilizing animals in which he described the animal kingdom as a revelation of the divine that should be protected and respected. He said that torture or cruelty to any animal was incompatible with normal human feelings and that it was not the role of the animal kingdom in the plan of creation to become the object of any kind of exploitation whatsoever.

How can such fundamental and contradictory statements from leading clergy and representatives of the Churches be explained? Are ordinary citizens and members of their congregations in particular perceived to have such short and easily manipulated memories that they can be denied any opinions of their own? Since those very strange statements in favour of the exploitation of our fellow creatures are regularly backed up by quotations from the Gospels it would seem necessary here to look somewhat more closely at the origins and development of the New Testament, which is most often quoted, and what it has to say that may be relevant to this matter.

Not so long ago, lay people were still described in ecclesiastical parlance as *idiotae*. To them the Bible was explained as being a homogeneous work handed down as though from heaven which in all its statements bore witness to the religion given and proclaimed to us by Jesus Christ and which only the Church was permitted to interpret. In the light of historical evolution both these statements are incorrect.

During the third century after Christ, the Church in Rome began to select from among countless manuscripts and descriptions a number of texts that had originated between AD 60 and AD 150. These selected texts then formed a canon that was to provide the foundation for the final compilation which included the four Gospels. However, the incomprehensibility of the very diverse contents on the one hand and the considerable variance between the conceptual definitions of the different authors on the other led to irreconcilable contradictions and incompatibilities. Endeavours to achieve some mutual alignment were then made, which even in the manuscripts involved comprehensive alterations to achieve standardization by means of omissions and additions as well as 'interpretative translations' that changed the meaning of the contents. Even under these circumstances it proved impossible to elaborate a uniform gospel that was free of any incomprehensible distortions of meaning. The works we now have before us make this understandable. It was therefore ultimately decided to retain the four Gospels and include the other texts. In this form the canon of the New Testament was then recognized under Pope Damasus in the year AD 382.

Since the original manuscripts of the Gospels are no longer extant, present-day commentaries rest on the Greek-language texts of the fourth century which were later translated several more times. Even during the nearly two centuries prior to the completion there had been an intense battle about and against the mostly older texts not included because their content was said to be incompatible with the selected four Gospels. This 'purge' led to the destruction of many irreplaceable works and manuscripts of fundamental Christian significance and content, isolated specimens of which had initially been preserved and thus saved in the old monastic libraries of the Near East. These were the Codices Cantabrigeniensis and the Codex Syrus-sinaiticus which, once found, helped in the compilation of the Agrapha. These comprised a compilation of the sayings and instructions of Jesus not included in the Gospels whereby use was made by the cleric Athanasus of the Codex sinaiticus and by Makarios the Great of the Codices of the Scythian Desert (according to Resch). Once they had been used and registered in the Agrapha these unique contemporary documents, too, were destroyed, while a publication of this collection remains outstanding to this day.

The introduction of the canon of the New Testament as the foundation of faith evidently caused problems. Thus a Church ruling was still required in the fifth century before the continuous narrative of Tatian (the *Diatessaron*), in use in the Near East, could be replaced by the four separate Gospels. (Hennecke.)

With regard to the historical origin of the four Gospels, which are surely the most important foundation of the New Testament, it is of significance that the oldest of these is said not to originate with the Apostle Mark but with Peter's interpreter in Rome. During his work for Peter he recorded everything he heard about the sayings and prophecies of Christ in a very precise and orderly manner. This Gospel originated before AD 70 although the conclusion was added much later.

Luke was a physician and as a healer it is likely that he maintained close links with the Essenes. According to the description in the Muratorian canon (AD 180 in Rome) he wrote his book after Christ's Ascension when Paul joined him and suggested he should do this.

The fourth Gospel was written by John because his fellow apostles urged him to do so. It had been revealed to Andrew that John should write down what he knew under his own name and that the others should check his written statements. Both these activities were to be undertaken after a period of fasting, and this is what was done.

The Gospel according to Matthew is the one most frequently mentioned. It cannot have been written before AD 70 because it refers to the destruction of Jerusalem at that time. Written in Aramaic, it is mostly based on older texts and contains most of the parables and instructions given by Jesus. What is remarkable about this Gospel is that in part it agrees entirely with the other three but in other respects also differs greatly from them.

Especially from the time when Christianity was made the state religion of the Roman Empire by Constantine the Great, the Gospels were again subjected to further alterations and adjustments with the aim of aligning and adapting the text and content of 'holy scripture' to what had become 'strictly of the faith' through the various changes that had occurred over the centuries. This work was done by certain scholars, the so-called *Correctores* who were appointed at the Council of Nicaea (AD 325) and then paid and supervised by the Church authorities. They carried out their duties for a long time and were particularly in demand when subsequent Councils or Conclaves repeatedly decided on important changes in matters of faith, so that the consequent discrepancies over against previous representations of Christian statements and their ecclesiastical interpretations could be avoided. (After Nestle.) Taking into account the destruction of so many codices and other available source works, the scale of these various corrections would probably never have become known had 'chance' not stepped in and put a spoke in the wheel of fate.

During the twentieth century, and more especially in its later decades, excavations in the Near East brought to light manuscripts and scrolls that are somewhat older than those of the Gospels and provide contemporary descriptions of what was going on in Palestine so long ago. Reading and translating them was not a problem since they were found to be in excellent condition. And as they had of course not undergone any 'correction' they provided revealing opportunities for comparative study. Known as 'Gospel fragments', they are in fact older than the recognized Gospel texts.

They turned out to be religious documents and manuscripts of epochal significance that had been buried for example in the rocky shore region of the Dead Sea or stored in caves, having originated at various times, in some cases reaching back to around 100 years before Christ. Scrolls were also discovered by a Bedouin whose goat had strayed into one of the numerous caves. They were stored in jars sealed with wax and pitch and their condition was similarly excellent. All the locations were in the vicinity of the Engeddi valley, which had been the main seat of the Essene community even in pre-Christian times. Numerous smaller monasteries had clustered around the main centre in which some of the brothers had even lived as hermits.

Only a few years after the first finds, 40 caves had been discovered in the area which yielded more than 250 further scrolls. The remains of impressively large buildings with adjacent structures and also cemeteries with countless graves harking back to that time were also found together with more documents in various languages, all of which confirmed the area as the centre of the Essene order that had covered the entire Near East.

The locations and circumstances of the finds and the significance of the scrolls gave cause for more research into the religious community of the Essenes and the influence on culture and lifestyle it had exerted over the region both before and after Christ. Its exact age is not known, but there is proof that about 100 years before Christ it was reorganized by an important initiate known as Jesu ben Pandira. He was the son of a Jewish woman and a Roman captain who saved her from death by stoning and spent the rest of his life with her.

Because of his life story and similar name, Jesu ben Pandira is frequently confused by other religions with Jesus of Nazareth who lived 100 years later. He was educated for many years in an Alexandrine Mystery school. Rules of the order originating from him may still be found in the apocryphal writings and partially even in the Gospels themselves.

John the Baptist and also Jesus of Nazareth were later closely associated with the Essenes. Today they would be termed accredited or honorary members. Both were admitted to the highest council of the order.

The community attached great importance to keeping their knowledge secret from outsiders but it was passed on gradually to members during their instruction. Contemporary descriptions confirm the most carefully guarded treasure as having been a number of sacred writings from which readings and teachings were given during gatherings. Despite being absolutely peace-loving, maintaining personal poverty and a strictly ascetic and vegetarian lifestyle, the Essenes had many enemies in the country and, like the Christians later on, were especially persecuted by the Maccabees on religious grounds.

After the time of Christ and in order to protect their documents and books against interference by forces inimical to the Mysteries and to prevent them from being altered, the Essenes often distributed them to the surrounding monasteries or hid them in the caves where they have now been found. The manner of this secure and well-maintained care allows us to draw conclusions as to the nature of their plans for the future.

At this point we must now correct a grave mistake in translation that has led to perceptions and interpretations about the Last Supper which clearly contradict Christian thought. In the usual editions of the New Testament it is claimed that the Last Supper consisted of an Easter lamb, which many interpret as proving that, unlike the Essenes, Christ Jesus cannot have been a vegetarian.

Anyone who is familiar with the Jewish laws of that time, however, will know that no Jew would have dared to slaughter a lamb on a Thursday, or even sell one or prepare a meal from it. This law was especially strict on the Thursday before the Passover, because that was the most important Jewish festival.

Perhaps the translation of the Gospels into Greek already contains some errors of interpretation. Nevertheless, there is no doubt that Luther translated the Greek word *to pas-kha* into 'paschal lamb' or 'Easter lamb'. And almost all later editions took their cue from this. Originally, and certainly in those times, however, the word meant 'Easter meal', which consisted of onions, bread and unfermented wine (grape juice). These ingredients were also described in detail, whereas the word 'lamb' is not mentioned anywhere. Not until much later was this concept extended to mean the Easter lamb or even the Easter festival. Luther's choice of words must thus be regarded as incorrect, which is also shown by the following considerations.

In the important Gospel of John the (Greek) term 'Easter meal' is not used at all, and in view of the moment in question being three days before Easter it could anyway not have been an Easter meal in the sense of *to pas-kha*. John used the word 'supper' in an unmistakable translation which makes the meaning quite clear.

Another important indicator [in Mark and Luke, Tr.] is the express mention of the man bearing a pitcher of water, in whose house the meal was to be prepared. Among the Essenes it was the husband who fetched water from the well, and the Essenes were strict vegetarians.

We may also mention here the summary concerning the relationship between human beings and the animals, the foundation of all Christian knowledge made by Christ during the washing of the feet before the Last Supper on the day preceding the Crucifixion: 'In this shall you recognize my followers, that they love one another and show compassion and love towards all God's creatures, especially those that are weak and oppressed, or persecuted although they are innocent. For all the earth is full of selfishness and ignorance, and of dark places of cruelty, pain and fear. I say to you again: Love one another and all God's creatures.'

This summary links our thoughts directly with an utterance by Francis of Assisi which is bound to stir even the most unwilling doubter to think about the Christian attitude to the animal kingdom: 'The animals are as much God's children as we are; so they are our brothers and sisters.'

The only document in the New Testament that contains a

recommendation concerning the eating of meat and the drinking of fermented (alcoholic) beverages is the first epistle of Paul to Timothy. We must here remember that normally the wine frequently mentioned in connection with the bread was not fermented grape juice. It was always a concentrated fruit juice that had to be diluted with water when imbibed. Even today, this method is used to make juice keep longer.

Apart from the recommendation to eat meat and drink alcohol, this first epistle to Timothy is written in a style that is not compatible with that of the second epistle, and in addition it contains the unusual feature of warning against the 'sect' of the Gnostics who are actually mentioned by name. One of the unalterable principles adhered to by the Gnostics as well as by their followers, the Severians, Eucratics and Apotactics, was the strict rule to abstain from eating meat, drinking fermented wine or possessing any property, which they justified on the basis of their own knowledge as well as the explicit assertions made by Jesus. They were not slow to point out the Church's deviations from this in what it did and said which, combined with other criticisms, made them very unpopular. Their unshakeable belief in matters of faith led to their being persecuted.

This epistle to Timothy was obviously intended to use Paul's authority to cover and legitimate the Church's interpretation while at the same time discrediting the religious interpretations and conduct of the Gnostics. The embarrassing point to be made here is the evident historical error in that at the time of the Apostle Paul no one was yet talking about the Gnostics, so that he would hardly have been warning against this 'sect'. (After W. Winsch.) It is interesting to note that among other things this epistle to Timothy is now used by Buddhists to prove the inferiority of Christianity in comparison with their own religion. The fact that it differs in form, content and style from the others, that the warning given in it is not compatible with historical fact, and that this is the only time when the consumption of alcohol and meat is recommended has persuaded important Church historians to declare this epistle to be a forgery.

St Basil the Great (AD 330–79), the famous Church Father and archbishop of Caesarea, a distinguished interpreter of Christian thought, described in his epistles the relationship between human beings and animals as follows: 'A human body burdened with meat dishes will be afflicted by illnesses. A moderate lifestyle will make it healthier and stronger by rooting out the problem at its source. The fumes arising from the eating of meat darken the light of the spirit. No matter what type of meat dishes fill the stomach, impurities arise and the soul becomes as though smothered beneath the burden of the food; it loses its ability to think. So long as one lives moderately the good fortune of one's house will increase, the animals will live in safety, no blood will be shed and no animals killed. The knife in the kitchen will be unused and the table set only with the fruits of nature.'

To follow these things up in detail would be pointless, and it would exceed the framework of our present considerations to try to fathom what reasons some might have had for distorting what the four Gospels say. But in view of the many admonishments that have been uttered during the course of the Church's history and the many proofs that exist of an attitude that is not in keeping with true Christian thought, it is justifiable to ask clearly and urgently whether the time has not come to reinstitute the office of the *Correctores*.

The purpose this time would be to make good the damage done and point to the overall meaning and credibility of the important content contained in the Gospels. Only once their meaning and content has been restored can they be seen as a binding foundation upon which Christian beliefs can be interpreted.

Christian thought should be known and acknowledged. It is contradictory to the Christian view to suggest or even teach for reasons of expediency that this thought is something other than what it really is.

7
Oriental Influences in the Sciences

There can scarcely be a field of human culture in which there are such differing and conflicting views and ideas as that of diseases and their cures. Especially in our day, with its orthodox medical views oriented entirely in accordance with science and involving animal experimentation and the allopathic treatment of disease, the difference between these attitudes and religious and philosophical considerations concerning the causes of diseases and ways of curing them appears to be unbridgeable. Present orthodox medical opinion also rejects the intermediate 'paramedical' therapies that are applied in many different ways around the world, as well as many indisputably successful natural healing methods the boundaries of which are, though, not clearly defined. It cannot be doubted that the mechanism by which these methods influence the sick body remains unexplained, but there are also no objective reasons for rejecting them.

Often the 'un-medical' yet frequent success of some healing methods is not acknowledged, and religious faith healings in particular are declared to be an 'inexplicable phenomenon'. Most people are quite satisfied with this while wilfully over-looking the even more astonishing question as to how, when medicine is so wonderfully researched and rationalized, there can be any room in it for unexplained phenomena. Seen objectively, surely even a single such 'unexplained healing' ought to be regarded as an inducement for a critical reappraisal of exclusively scientific medical ideas, with the definition 'unexplained' being regarded as unsatisfactory. If both orthodox medicine and paramedical methods have some therapeutic successes while remaining unable to cure every disease, then one should conclude that both have a basis of effectiveness that is not yet fully explained.

Setting aside the competitiveness that of course exists between the two, what is the cause of their mutually incompatible conceptions and what are the deeper reasons for their mutual lack of understanding? It will be necessary to examine the distant past of medical history in order to find a satisfactory and irrefutable explanation. This will not only mean referring to current historical research into the separate therapeutic paths that have been followed, for it will also be necessary to view these in conjunction with the influence of the spiritual sciences and developments of a religious and philosophical nature. Medicine especially was originally guided by such influences, and almost all traditional healing wisdom stems from the ancient Mystery schools.

Furthermore, power politics has played its part not only in influencing the direction thinking has taken but also in the long-term establishment of cultural impulses by organizations not always noticeable to the public eye and aimed at influencing the development of human culture over several generations.

As we know, our present university education in all disciplines and especially in the sciences was introduced in the early Middle Ages by the Arabs residing in the South and West and taken over with various changes by Europe as it developed. In the western world the ways of thinking established then still today provide the basis and thought structure of all scientific views and current academic teaching methods.

What is not so well known is that this type of scientific attitude towards the world and the role played by human beings in it did not stem from the Arabs at all but was adopted by them during their campaigns and wars in the Near East. It stemmed from Gundishapur in Mesopotamia, which was the highest seat of learning both before and after the time of Christ. The learning the Arabs acquired there was of course changed and adapted in accordance with their own ideas and inclinations. But the learning itself, a predominantly medical and scientific view of the world, was also contributed to over the centuries by scholars expelled from other parts of the world, including the Roman Empire and the regions belonging to it, especially Greece.

The various rulers of Gundishapur must be credited with having gathered, catalogued and registered the totality of human knowledge and wisdom from the Mysteries in the most important of the disciplines of medicine, chemistry, philosophy and astronomy. Tremendous efforts and expenditure were made in creating universities and gigantic libraries for the purpose of disseminating the knowledge and wisdom. The art of healing was taught as the highest field of learning, and students were first expected to acquire extensive knowledge of all the sciences, astronomy, astrology, philosophy, religion, and spiritual and esoteric matters. All this knowledge was considered to belong together as a foundation for practising the art of healing successfully in combination with the right attitude to the human being. Physicians were the most revered of professionals because their art rested not only on knowledge of all the laws of nature but also on a special intuitive skill that was needed in order to diagnose an illness and then heal the sick person.

The spiritual centre of Gundishapur sent its influence over to Europe right into the Middle Ages. How it came into being can only be explained when one considers all the cultural currents of the ancient and modern world that existed within the Roman Empire and were also working against it. During the early centuries after the Event at Golgotha, Christian thought forms with very different social ideas began to exert a strong influence from the South. Since these ideas were taken up among the Germanic tribes relatively early on and received support from Irish sources, a considerable spiritual force also began to work into the centre of the Roman Empire from the North as well. At the same time increasingly occult forces of an oriental kind began to impinge threateningly on the stability of the Empire from the East.

So whereas, while Christ was still on the earth, the Roman emperors were looking with concern towards the North, in the third century a 'Persian threat' began to menace them from the East, from Gundishapur. Meanwhile Rome itself, as the centre of the great Empire it had acquired by conquest, was showing ever more signs of what would later lead to its downfall. The emperors themselves also began to realize their weaknesses and endeavoured increasingly to obtain knowledge and support from Persia's great Sun Mystery. Drawn thither as though by magic, the emperors appeared one after another before Heliogabalus, the high priest of the Sun Temple at Emesa, seeking to save their internally and externally waning political power with the support of the ancient Persian Mystery wisdom.

Thus it was that the spiritual atmosphere of Persia came to enjoy world-wide renown. This reached its peak in the third century in the Mithras Mysteries, which represented a renaissance of a changed and no longer relevant further development of the ancient Persian, Zarathustrian sun religion.

At this very time, instructed and guided by its priests and

magicians, the legendary Ardashir, a grandson of the famous King Sassan, overthrew the ruling dynasty of the Parthian kings in Mesopotamia and established the Sassanid kingdom which later came to be guided by the same priest-magicians. As its power and influence increased it became a serious threat to the Roman Empire. Shapur I (242–72), the second Sassanid king, brought the Empire to the edge of the abyss when his troops penetrated into Syria and up to the Mediterranean where, in AD 262, they sacked the city of Antioch and captured the Emperor Valerian. During these campaigns Shapur founded a number of towns where he immediately resettled the deported inhabitants of Antioch. The largest and most important of these was named after him: Gundishapur. It attained world renown for centuries and became the second capital of the Sassanid kingdom. All that remains today are extensive ruins known as Beth-Lapat or Lapeta.

For a long period it was the seat of the priest-magicians who had adopted the ancient and profound wisdom of Zarathustra and revived it in an outdated form in that it had not undergone the spiritual transformation brought into the world by the Christian impulse. In order to increase their power they interwove the ancient Mystery wisdom of Ahura Mazda with that of the sun cult of the Sassanids in a fatal entanglement. As a result, what in pre-Christian times had existed to serve the Christ-impulse became after the time of Christ a movement that opposed Christianity and manifested as the impulse of Gundishapur.

This development led to the manifestation of a terrible omen when the great initiate Mani ventured to point out to King Shapur I that he was following a path which was no longer of the age. Mani had to flee, and when he returned after many years in India, China and other countries the

Sassanids accused him of blasphemy. The reigning King Bahram I had him crucified after which his stuffed skin was hung up above the city gates. His Manichaean followers had their heads buried in the ground.

In addition to demonstrating profound Gnostic and esoteric knowledge, such actions also gave a glimpse of a fundamental opposition to Christ and the bearing this was to have on how humanity would fare in the future.

For centuries the Hellenic culture and attitude of mind had spread throughout the Mediterranean region, and Alexandria had become its capital. All the sciences were cultivated there including those pertaining to the cosmos. The main disciplines of medicine, theosophy, chemistry, astronomy, biology and theology were imbued with the profound wisdom of the Gnostics and Aristotelian thought. All the sciences, which in those days still linked heaven and earth, were mutually compatible and complementary to one another on that basis.

Such trends of thought and any concepts resulting from them were in opposition to the interests and opinions of the Roman emperors who thus came to be considered barbarians because of their rejection, not only in Greece, of any independent spiritual development. So the immensely learned academic world with all its inestimable cultural manifestations was gradually rooted out by Roman imperialism, with those who represented it being driven eastwards by arbitrary measures and persecution. Although Constantine decreed in AD 324 that Christianity was to be the state religion, ordering the closure of heathen temples and threatening 'pagan superstition' with the death sentence, nevertheless he was the sole arbiter as to what constituted 'heathenness', and his measures militated unambiguously against Aristotelian ways of thinking and teaching. The famous Eleusinian Mysteries

were banned and Hypatia, a philosopher of genius and fol-
lower of Aristotle, was allowed to be torn to pieces on the
street by the crowds without any interference from authority.
The Persian Academy at Edessa was closed down and the last
and greatest Apollo Temple on Monte Cassino was destroyed
together with its equally famous library. Constantine's suc-
cessor Justinian I closed down Plato's Academy in Athens
and deprived all the teachers not only of their salaries but of
any form of state support, in many cases by denying them
their citizens' rights.

The persecuted and outlawed scientists, scholars, philosophers and initiates were forced to flee. The sciences and wisdom banished with them found refuge, protection and the
possibility to develop further among the Persians, the arch-
enemies of the Romans.

All the important knowledge and scientific achievements
were thus lost to the western world. And when the great
library in Alexandria with its irreplaceable treasury of wisdom was destroyed by arson, the temple of wisdom built up
by the greatest and most inspired intellects of the age col-
lapsed in ruins. Initially a great deal of the wisdom fell victim
to oblivion. A hopeless desert of the spirit was bequeathed to
the future by the Roman emperors, with Justinian being
perhaps the worst culprit.

King Shapur II was a contemporary of the Emperor Julian.
He welcomed every scientist and cultivated culture and science. He had the famous medical works of the Greek Christian physician Theodore translated, and thus, in combination
with many other books, all the Persian, Indian and Greek
therapeutic wisdom reached Gundishapur, including the
medical knowledge of Hippocrates. That his teachings are
still known today is due to the Sassanid kings. By the fourth

century the Academy had at its disposal the esoteric medical knowledge of all the ancient Mysteries which formed the foundation of that wonderful medical wisdom that spread out into the world from there for a very long time and formed the basis for every medical idea.

The later Persian king Khosru Anushirvan (532–80), a pupil of the famous Greek scholar Stephanos of Byzantium, became a patron of the Academy and especially of the medical sciences. Because the decisions he made were often very important, this genuine philosopher and initiate is sometimes erroneously named as the founder of Gundishapur. He not only summoned Indian and Chinese scholars to his university, which had grown to encompass several thousand students, but also continued to grant expelled scholars the right to remain in his land and supported their professional existence. Emperor Justinian I (527–65) was his contemporary and spiritual antagonist who, as we have mentioned, did everything in his power to drive science and wisdom from Europe to Asia. His brutal edicts and laws, which deprived all 'non-Christians' and heretics including Manichaeans and Nestorians of their rights or else banished them or even threatened them with death, succeeded during his reign in driving every last bearer of Hellenistic temple wisdom to the Sassanid protectors of the sciences.

On the surface, for the comprehension of the common people, these measures were directed at the so-called heretics, including Manichaeans and Nestorians, who did not want to bow down to the might of the Roman emperors but represented a Christian understanding of the world. The actual targets, however, were the representatives of the Platonic world view and way of thinking, and also the Aristotelians. That is why so many philosophers and scientists were among those who fled or emigrated. Of these, mention is nowadays made only of Damascius, Simplicius, Eulamius, Philoponus, Uranius, Diogenes, Hermias, Priscionus, Isidorus and other pupils of the initiates Ammonius and Iamblichus.

All the important and rare works were catalogued at the Academy of Gundishapur after the Hellenistic and Indian Gnostic ones had been translated into Syrian and other languages. There were two famous medical scientists with the necessary knowledge who served King Khosru as translators: the Indian physician Burzoe and the Syrian priest and physician Sargis of Risaina who had been trained in Alexandria. They translated, commented and catalogued all the scientific and alchemical works of the ancient world, all the publications by Plato and Aristotle, Dionysus the Areopagite and well-known Greek physicians who had knowledge and experience from the Mystery centres. All the cultural knowledge of the world at that time thus came to be taken up into the cultural centre where everything that contributed to the traditional knowledge of human history was being collected. This was the greatest and most influential period of an antiquated Zoroastrian Mystery wisdom that had failed to absorb the earth's Christian impulse. It was also its final manifestation on the physical plane.

A mighty army of Arabs filled with enthusiasm began its conquests up from the South into the Persian realm. Driven by religious fanaticism, the movement initiated by the visionary Mohammed (571–632) was powerful enough, arriving in Persia via Egypt and Syria, to destroy the mighty ancient Persian Mysteries and powers. In 635 they conquered Damascus and Jerusalem, and in 641 Alexandria and Gundishapur. Where Hellenism and Arabism had formerly opposed one another there now arose a new source in world history of spiritual and cultural energy and vigour founded on the mixture of Greek knowledge and Arabian wisdom. But the original impulse had not perished but began a new transformed flowering supported by caliph Yezed ben Mu'awiya. The Syrian monk Marianus had initiated the caliph into the triad of the sciences of medicine, alchemy and astrology, which persuaded him, as the first Muslim in history, to translate the existing collected works of wisdom—especially those of the Greeks into Arabic.

Thus the riches of world-wide Gnostic wisdom entered into Arabian culture whence Arab conquests later carried it to France and England in its Muslim form. Two of the most famous esotericists of all time were Al-Jafar, who stemmed from Damascus in the eighth century and, a hundred years later, the equally erudite Al-Jabir (Latin, Geber). Until well into the eighteenth century the latter was regarded in Europe as a unique authority on alchemy who exercised a fundamental influence on all the sciences. He was perhaps one of the greatest and most universal scholars of the Orient who brought the esoteric sciences of the East over to the West, whereby especially astrology and alchemy as Arabian disciplines from Mesopotamia were absorbed particularly by the scholars of the therapeutic sciences.

Several providential events recorded in history were decisive for the continuation and promotion of the Academy under Islamic rule. Having been given up for lost by traditional Arabian medicine, a number of fatally sick caliphs had subsequently been cured by physicians brought to their aid from Gundishapur, and in consequence the Academy was allowed to continue in existence over a long period.

Arabian culture and science attained unequalled celebrity under Harun al-Rashid (786–809) and al-Ma'Mun (813–30).

It would be hard to find other rulers who did as much for science, culture and the arts, whereby all the academic achievements were exclusively applied for the welfare of contemporary humanity. Once again the greatest interest was directed towards medical knowledge. Harun al-Rashid established hospitals, observatories, libraries and universities. The state paid for hosts of scholars to journey all over the world, including China, Africa, India and even Schleswig Holstein in Germany, in order to study and purchase scientific writings.

Most books were translated into all the known languages of the age, and the importance attached to medical literature may be concluded from such names as Hippocrates, Dioscorides, Galen, Alexander of Tralles, Setgios and Gurgios Bocht-Jeshu.

In this way the stream of ancient Greek scholarship and culture flowed into Arabian culture with the aid of the teachers of Gundishapur. Taken up by the Semitic Arabs who tended to be intellectually abstract in their thinking, the Gnostic wisdom was transformed in order to be fitted into the spirit of the Arabian language which was foreign to Greek philosophy, Aristotelian thought forms and esoteric knowledge. The result was an unnatural mingling of the mature and ancient wisdom of Imagination with the cool and calculating intellectuality of the Semites who accepted only the validity of their astute sense perceptions which they overlaid with the flourishing fantasy of their desert blood and the dazzling religious visions of their Prophet. Not much was left of the original knowledge of the spirit that lies behind and within matter, nor of the influences that had once been felt to come from the beyond, because these had to make way for 'more rational' perceptions.

This, then, was the changed atmosphere of Gundishapur under the Arabs where outstanding scholarship continued to flourish, but now only on the basis of what could be perceived by the senses in the material world. This scholarship was to confront the human being's 'intellectual soul' many centuries before it had matured sufficiently; and the still only delicately germinating 'I' would be dazzled by materialistic achievements while what should have been its regular development was prevented.

This Arabian Persian science was characterized by two prominent but very different components. Initially the traditional esoteric Gnostic approach continued, but in a changed form. The true way to understand this approach is from the point of view of the supersensible, for it is from this angle that the forces at work in matter can be perceived. But as a consequence of the Arabian way of thinking an entirely opposite element then began to develop in all the scientific disciplines. This was the method of observing and experimenting which, though very acute, is based solely on sense perceptions while ignoring influences coming from the spirit and being satisfied with investigating only physically perceptible phenomena.

With the constant neglect of the spiritual side of knowledge leading to the spirit becoming totally forgotten, humanity was increasingly left with 'observing nature', the only form of scientific research now remaining. Building on this, the medical sciences came to regard animals as being the same as humans, which meant that they could be used as 'models' for research into human diseases and therapies. By their translations of all Greek scientific and esoteric thinking, the two Syrian physicians Yachya ben Massaveh and Ishaq ben Hunain introduced the Arabian way of thinking into

Gundishapur. The two ways of thinking were already beginning to show in them. For example Hunain on the one hand published works showing him to be a theosophist or esotericist, whereas on the other hand the first historically documented examples of work involving vivisection as a means of research are attributed to him, a method that is irreconcilable with being an esotericist.

He made a compilation of philosophical mottoes that contained a great many purely pagan philosophical meditations. The selectivity in his choice of authors revealed his problematical and disapproving relationship with Christianity, which no doubt arose out of the different view of the world held by this Arab who sought to enlighten.

So by the time of the ninth century we find all the neo-Platonists being translated into Arabic, but almost no writings of Christian knowledge or thought. Anything imbued with a Christian impulse which could help human beings develop in a healthy way or which contained more advanced messages about their position in the cosmos was eliminated from the body of wisdom taught.

More and more the search for knowledge was directed only towards sensual observation of the physical world. Meanwhile the cosmic and spiritual forces as the system that shapes and organizes matter and biological functions was increasingly left out of knowledge until it was forgotten altogether.

Despite this, especially in the medical field taught at the Academy, much excellent work was done in relation to the human body showing not only by anatomical, physiological or surgical dissection how it could be seen as a totality guided from within, although without any connection being made between this inner guidance and the spiritual worlds. The main branches of the art of healing had now become the pharmacology of plants, dietary insights, and uroscopy, by which was meant diagnosis based on inspection of urine, since this provides a comprehensive view of the organism's metabolic processes.

It was known that the chemistry of the human body differed fundamentally from that of other life forms. More advanced Mystery knowledge was familiar with the ways in which the organs of the human body and their functions and also the functions of animals, plants and natural substances are linked with the formative planetary forces that determine and shape them.

We may add here that in those days the planets were not conceived of in abstract terms but were seen to be spiritual beings belonging to the heavenly hierarchies. This ancient wisdom harked back to the knowledge from the various Mysteries originally gathered at Gundishapur, where it provided the foundation for the art of healing as well as for alchemy, astrology and philosophy. All of these were seen as belonging together as one body of knowledge essential for the diagnosis and cure of human diseases.

From conception to death, and regulated by the ether body, all the forces and substances of the physical world stream through the organism in the form of nourishment, metabolism and excretion. The etheric and spiritual principles were regarded as the healthy part of the human being, while the transition through the body of foreign physical substances was seen as possibly leading to sickness. The art of healing aimed both to maintain health and if need be to restore it by means of suitable diet and phytotherapeutic medication. However, it was only permissible for the teacher to divulge orally the ultimate experiences and secrets to pupils who were deemed to have the right attitude and be suitably receptive.

But even the knowledge recorded in books reveals the depth of medical understanding of cosmic laws and the etheric principle of the human being. Travelling with the Arabian influence via northern Africa to Spain and France, the medical knowledge arriving there proved to be superior to what was locally known and was adapted to suit local cultures. So right into the sixteenth century the people of Europe were treated almost exclusively by healing methods that had come from Gundishapur.

The influence exercised by this impulse from the Mesopotamian Academy right into the Middle Ages is shown by the statutes of the medical faculty of the University of Vienna dated 1389, which remained valid until the middle of the fifteenth century: 'Every scholar desiring to attain the baccalaureate must provide evidence that he has studied the first and fourth books of Avicenna's *Canon of Medicine*, the ninth book of al-Razi, and the *Ars commentatae* of Johannitius [or Hunain].'

Despite the work of Constantine the African who, after long years spent in Africa and the East, founded a school of Arabian medicine at Salerno which supplied the whole of Italy with physicians, despite the equally well-known physicians al-Razi and Avicenna who worked in Spain and France, despite the various academic chairs of the great philosopher and physician Ibn Roshd and his equally successful pupil Musa ben Meimum, not least despite the work of the physician and initiate Averroes (1126–98) and his work *Colliget*, a complete handbook of Arabian medicine, and also despite the genius of the physicians and teachers Abu Sahl, al-Fabiri and Isa ben Jahja, it took only a few centuries before oblivion overtook the corrected medical knowledge about the human being that had been passed down. The new sciences sought to research the human being and his environment on the basis of materialism.

The long-established links between the human being and the kingdoms of nature that surround him were forgotten, as were the therapeutic possibilities arising from them. He was studied in isolation from his environment, and his links with the cosmos were no longer recognized. This was the beginning of what today has culminated in scientific thinking that denies any conception of the human organism as being a part of creation as a whole.

The organism was divided up into separate parts and functions and this became the basis on which physiology was studied. There was no recognition or explanation of the way the different processes functioned. The consequences of this were research methods that were purely experimental and physical, whereby human beings and animals were treated as equivalents while the differences between them were no longer grasped.

The second century after Christ saw the first sweeping change when everything of a Christian nature, and therefore the influence of Christianity as such, was eliminated from the Mystery wisdom gathered at Gundishapur. Thereafter the remnants of elementary knowledge about the cosmic structure of the human being and his relationship with the powers of creation gradually sank into complete oblivion during the course of the early and later Middle Ages. The once tremendous knowledge brought back to Europe by the Arabs via its detour to Gundishapur thus came to bear little resemblance to its original Gnostic Greek and esoteric Christian wisdom.

Science today is quite right in regarding its source as stemming from traditional Arabian scientific and therapeutic concepts, but it is incapable of evaluating the change of quality that has occurred in the interim. The research attitude that has meanwhile arisen is able only to train the intellectual capacity to form concepts. But it cannot experience the deeper knowledge that takes in humanity's links with the spiritual world; nor does it mediate the necessary wisdom for this. The modes of thinking that entered European culture have held human beings back from insight into the real spiritual world and have too early brought forward the development of the intellect, which can only encompass nature in its physical manifestations.

Tendencies such as these have led to an unconscious arrogance that senses and uses the might of the intellect without being able to perceive its inability to penetrate with understanding to knowledge about the spiritual world. The science of our time can thus readily confirm material reality but can no longer grasp its real spiritual background. Science of this kind can erect impressive systems of perceptions and concepts about the sense-perceptible world but cannot mediate any insight into the spiritual forces that shape this world.

The final result was a fundamental change in the understanding of the human being's place in creation which degraded him to a mere earthly animal. Thus he was denied not only any personal spirituality but also any capacity for higher knowledge. Not only a productive power of thought that could penetrate into spiritual realms was denied him, but also the existence of his immortal 'I'. All that was granted to him was the ability to entertain earthbound, sensory and physical concepts.

However, wherever cosmic forces interfere in human destiny in ways that are not in keeping with evolution helpful protectors are also not far away. Thus in the Middle Ages there arose a great transforming impulse that was capable of banishing the corrupting forces when from the arsenal of Aristotle's genius the deeply Christian individual Thomas Aquinas (1225–74) began to forge weapons against the untimely Arabian conception of science. By correcting the false interpretations about human thinking and existence he proved the existence of the cosmic and spiritual human self.

Much later Rudolf Steiner described this individual spiritual principle that exists in the fully mature human being as that which raises him above the animals and thus lays the foundation for his responsibility towards all creatures and creation itself. The human 'I' experiencing itself in intuitive thinking thus experiences the power and freedom of Christ.

8
The Variety of Diseases and their Causes

Sickness and disease, as well as healing, have a profound effect on human life, and there is an increasing urgency about the questions of destiny to which they give rise. Why has this person suddenly fallen ill without any apparent reason, and why with this illness and not that one? A satisfactory explanation can only be found through insight into the living structure of the human being and his overall development. Since animals are not comparable either in their structure or in their life expectancy or reactions, inflicting diseases on them cannot lead to any understanding of this problem in humans.

The human being as a threefold entity consisting of a spirit, a soul and a body has been described in varying degrees of differentiation in important religious and philosophical documents in more recent times. It is significant that for millennia this knowledge has remained firmly embedded not only in every culture but also in the understanding and ideas of individuals. Even modern scientific thought has not turned away from these concepts, although the spirit can be neither measured nor reproduced, while the soul is only recognized from the medical point of view on occasions when a disease caused by it in the biological organism cannot be explained in terms of physiology or chemistry. For science, only the physical body exists, yet even here neither the totality of its functions nor the concept of 'life' in all its many forms can be fully explained.

Apart from a few exceptions, people on the whole make

little effort to enter more deeply into the higher principles of a living being or to examine statements concerning them from viewpoints other than those of logic or utility.

Within the visible body there is an organizational principle that is responsible for functions that are ceaselessly repeated, and for growth and recuperation. This is variously termed the 'life body', the 'ether body' or also the 'body of formative forces', all of which are used to describe one and the same system of energy. Human beings share the elementary basis of their ether body with animals and plants. It has to be seen as an organized, formed and precisely defined system of forces. Within this, and in addition to it there is the astral body, which human beings have in common—although not as an exact equivalent—only with the higher animals. The astral body makes it possible for there to be feelings involving the psyche. Finally, the human being's spirit is also described as the 'I'. This lifts us above all else that has evolved.

The general term 'sickness' or 'disease' is used to describe any disturbance in the way these strengthening, invigorating, feeling and self-aware functions work together. People usually only concern themselves with the cause, type or form of a disease when pain or indisposition impairs their fitness or efficiency. And when they visit the doctor their main interest is in getting better as quickly and painlessly as possible. In many cases they are not at all bothered about 'how' this is to be achieved. They also find it important to have to bear as little responsibility as possible personally for this and hope that they will not be required to change their lifestyle.

This way of thinking and behaving has resulted in a belief in medical authority that is far stronger than any former belief in religious authority. Interested circles have brought about the establishment of a 'medical papacy' in our society that never existed so strongly in earlier times.

Many researchers and medical experts whose way of thinking has been formed by contemporary scientific concepts are unaware, for example, that blood has quite different characteristics within or outside the many-layered systems of a living creature. When it leaves its species-specific etheric, astral or spiritual spheres of influence it changes most of the ways in which it functions. The 'I' especially has its field of influence in the blood where it brings about an individual immunity in each case.

The soul body or astral body manifests in or relates especially to the whole medium of the nervous system. For science this comprises the vegetative and sympathetic nervous systems with all their ganglia, and the central nervous system consisting of cerebrum, brain stem, cerebellum and spinal marrow. The conscious and unconscious manifestations of the spiritual personality or 'I', which exist in this form only in the human being, are registered, coordinated and transported via these many-layered and complex nerve links. In addition, the person's mood and other psychological effects are taken in and perceived, worked through inwardly and passed on to the biological functions.

This is where forces that are either in keeping with or unfavourable to evolution can enter in. In the form of moods, views and feelings they make their way to the soul via the so-called 'subconscious'. They work in the physiological realm by means of the nervous system and this is made visible as a reaction or the behaviour of an organism.

In a similar way the entire glandular system in its numerous functions is the physical counterpart of the species-specific ether body. The results can be analysed chemically, but the causes cannot be traced in this way. At this level the effectiveness and reactions are individual.

Although it is not always possible to distinguish medically between tendency and causation, by far the greater part of all illnesses are actually the consequence of environmental influences, nicotine and alcohol consumption or inappropriate diet, or accidents and their aftermath. They can thus be interpreted in connection with gradual or rapid damage to the organism through foreign substances ingested or external influences suffered. The time and manner in which the illness manifests and the course it follows depend, among other things, on the strength of the body's immune system.

Diseases that are caused by irregularities or interferences involving the human principle described as the 'I' usually manifest in its physical counterpart, the blood. These are usually chronic illnesses that make themselves felt clinically through symptoms in various parts of the body. But their deeper origins must be sought in the blood, or else in the 'I', which represents the individual in its totality. They are especially frequent in people who are dissatisfied with life and unable to come to grips with difficulties at work or in the family, or elsewhere.

Such patients tend never to feel quite well and experience their indisposition in all sorts of ways to such an extent that their ability to cope is heavily impaired. It is usually then not long before specific symptoms of some disease appear. The main reason for this lies in the way the nature of the individual concerned interacts with external influences and lifestyle. The individual's personal attitude to life's problems and destiny also plays an important part.

Once this has been diagnosed as being the case, treatment can include recognition of the patient's basic character and qualities, tendencies and wishes, i.e. some form of psychotherapy directed to the individual. Medical treatment of the symptoms by themselves might help in the short term but would not have a lasting effect. It would not take long for other symptoms to appear which would be due to the same underlying cause even if medically they were to be regarded as new symptoms.

A permanent cure would require the patient to reach a fundamental understanding of himself and perhaps also an assessment of his professional circumstances. This should not lead to extra psychological strain. Psychological care linked to the introduction of a rhythmical daily routine would be necessary over a longer period.

Many more acute forms of disease are caused predominantly by disorders of the astral body. The astral system is the initiator and bearer of passions, wishes and urges—in short, of the individual's entire emotional life. Its function is impaired by unsuitable lifestyles, negative thought patterns and bad external influences including unsuitable diet. It often takes some time before the symptoms are transferred to the physical body. When impulses are insufficiently worked through by the nervous system, various complaints can manifest, or even symptoms of acute illness throughout the whole body.

This does not mean to say that this is the cause, for example, of every stomach complaint. But if the cause does emanate from the astral principle, then treating the symptoms alone will have little effect.

Even orthodox medicine is beginning to recognize psychosomatic or neuro-vegetative causes of disease, but it does not differentiate these sufficiently or treat them thoroughly enough. Tranquillizers or psychosomatic medications are not suitable in such instances. They do not treat the causes of the disease, and by subduing or even destroying the will they prevent any normalizing self-healing. It is difficult to limit the dimensions or delayed consequences of such medications, which can take the form of impediments to impulse conduction or also functional or behavioural disorders or even alterations of character.

Since nutrition also plays an important part in causing these forms of disease, changes in diet can be advisable in addition to natural remedies and psychotherapy. During the course of evolution, human beings have become separated from the mineral and plant kingdoms, but these can still be effective and can therefore be used therapeutically.

In former times our predecessors still had a great store of knowledge about these links. They regarded medicinal herbs as living nature-beings with whom they could communicate and to whom they could entrust themselves. They sought help from them for someone who was sick. Trusting in them, they implored them to lend their healing forces, as still happens among unspoilt tribes to this day.

A sick person may be carried many hundreds of kilometres to a well-known medicine man who is asked to find out whether the illness has been caused by poisoning due to eating the wrong food or indigestible plants, or whether it is the result of 'violating the laws of the ancestors'. If the former is the case, the patient is sent on to another medicine man who prescribes a phytotherapeutic treatment and dietary measures. In the latter case treatment is considerably more difficult, since help has to be sought from deceased ancestors who still occupy a position of leadership and assistance within the tribe. This is done, for example, by means of ritual dances.

It can happen that certain acute or chronic diseases occur

frequently within an ethnic group where they manifest as functional disorders of the glandular system. These are connected with the ether body. It is characteristic of these disorders that usually several organs or organ functions are affected either all at once or one after the other.

In former times the activity of the life or ether body was felt to be linked with the influences of the stars and planets. In this sense the heart was related to the influence of the sun, the brain to the moon, the spleen to Saturn, the liver to Jupiter, the gall bladder to Mars, the kidneys to Venus, and the lungs to Mercury. They are also related to certain plants and minerals, which is why these can be used therapeutically to exercise a balancing influence. This can be especially successful if the disorder is partially caused by what might be called the character of a particular tribe or population.

Overall, externally similar symptoms may have their causes on different levels, which is why therapies must vary in different cases. An individual's own powers have a part to play in healing just as they also contribute to a person's disposition to a particular illness.

A perhaps more minor though important point to be made is that diseases relating to causes in the astral body usually involve strong pain, whereas those connected to the ether body are frequently pain-free to begin with but can cause discomfort later if complications occur or other organs become involved.

The treatment methods sketched for the disease groups mentioned are of course only successful when they are correctly applied in good time. Often, however, the disease has progressed to a stage where either allopathic medication with its side or subsequent effects or even surgery is needed. In the latter case the symptoms often remain the same or are merely displaced, which shows that the etheric or astral causes have not been addressed.

There is also another type of disease the causes of which initially appear to lie exclusively in the physical body. Apart from poisoning or accidents, this category includes all forms of infectious diseases. Leaving aside the possible need for treatment of the symptoms, at a deeper level what is needed is knowledge of the connections the human organism has with nature and the environment, and acceptance of the spiritual background of all physical phenomena.

For a long time there have been substantial reservations stating that various vaccinations transgress against the Hippocratic oath. The possible protection of a child against a low possibility of contracting an infectious disease does not, it is said, justify the risk of condemning an individual to lifelong problems with seizures caused by the vaccination, or becoming a brain-damaged invalid needing lifelong care. Since vaccination does indeed cause such damage to a numerically known extent, it should really be seen as a violation of the most ancient medical principle: not to cause harm.

This is not the only medical discipline in which physicians are restricted by law in their freedom to use their own discretion. When a type of therapy is prescribed, not using a 'scientifically recognized' therapy such as a vaccination could lead to legal consequences. Meanwhile, since the legislature is usually not prepared to be held responsible for the consequences of the vaccinations it prescribes, these being difficult to prove, those who are damaged by them stand little chance of receiving at least some financial compensation, except in a few heavily contested exceptional cases.

In the context of knowledge about human evolution

gleaned from spiritual science we must add that there are also forms of illness in which karmic factors can play a part either as results of past attitudes and actions or as a basis for future tasks and activities.

Knowledge about the role of karmic factors in diseases should be a part of the qualifying store of knowledge of every medical doctor. In many cases these are illnesses that do not respond to treatment and some are cases in which sudden death occurs without any apparent reason.

Unlike humans, the higher, warm-blooded animals possess only the three lower principles of their being on the earth, and in the cold-blooded lower creatures only the two lowest systems are at work. This being the case, there can be no doubt from this point of view that animal and human reactions are incompatible.

Paracelsus still possessed a great deal of knowledge and exceptional capabilities in these matters which even in his day caused him a great deal of trouble owing to the lack of understanding present in the orthodox medicine of the time. Despite, or perhaps on account of, his exceptional successes he was accused of being a dreamer, fantasist or charlatan. The end of this confrontation between ancient wisdom and 'modern' knowledge came in 1541 in Salzburg where he died a painful death in an inn after having been left lying untended for three days with a fractured skull after an accident. One biographer recorded that academic personal physicians, surgeons and even barbers stood beside his grave without distinction of their differences in rank and with a rare show of unanimity in their delight at his demise.

Being magnanimous in his physician's heart, he showed understanding and forgiveness despite everything when he wrote: 'I am no refined or subtle man who has dined at the tables of the great. My upbringing was rough and ready and I ate cheese and milk and oatmeal bread. May I therefore be forgiven if my speech does not always sound distinguished, for what I say is honestly meant and my only aim is to serve others!'

It is of course not my intention here to speak in favour of reviving the medicine of bygone ages. After all, both the make-up of the human being and external circumstances have all changed since then. Nevertheless, it would be in the interest of medicine on the one hand and of the animals on the other to apply a more objective and expert judgement to fundamental esoteric knowledge and to include it in the formulation of present-day concepts. When will science and research acknowledge with a little more modesty in their patterns of thought that all knowledge is subject to a continuous process of further development?

Part Two

RESPONSIBLE MEDICINE BASED ON A SPIRITUAL VIEW OF CREATION

9

Our Evolutionary Sibling Relationship with the Animals

Almost all religions, but especially the best-known Christian observer of the relationship between man and animal, St Francis of Assisi, tell us of a common ancestry of both these earth-dwellers. He said that our fellow creatures are just as much God's children as we are, in other words: our brothers and sisters.

In former times the wisdom of creation was taught in the Mystery schools only to those especially trained to receive it. But now Rudolf Steiner has made this knowledge available to all those willing to undertake some inner work on themselves to overcome any difficulties they might initially have. He has passed on to us the purest and most comprehensive knowledge about not only the past evolution of humanity but also what is to come in the future. He also spoke about the kingdoms of nature on the earth and the solar system with which they are linked, as well as the divine spiritual beings at work on these known in ecclesiastical parlance as the hierarchies of angels. His teachings also contain the most comprehensive information available today about the relationship between man and animal so that this knowledge can flow into our relationship with the environment in a truly Christian sense as the moral and ethical basis of our attitude to life.

The only explanation for the genesis of the universe is that it arose out of activities carried on by the most supreme divine beings. Plans for every new cosmic system arise out of the sphere of the Trinity that is above that of the angelic hierarchies. Seraphim receive them, Cherubim build them with wisdom, and Thrones shape them into reality through sacrifice. In doing so they relinquished a part of their physical manifestation, which was warmth, in what is now termed the 'Saturn stage' of our earth.

In this earliest phase of our planetary system's development the first beginnings of human physical bodies came into being. Later the original animal shapes split off from these in the astral plane, the ancestors of today's bees, ants and other insects that live in highly developed and differentiated social structures. Other animal forms had not yet begun to appear.

Just as human beings pass from incarnation to incarnation in order to live one life after another on the earth, so did our planet itself live through several incarnations before reaching its present state. All beings in both the greater and the lesser world are subject to the law of reincarnation. In between they disappear in what we could call a 'death' just as we do when we relinquish our physical form. In the case of the planetary stages this invisible state is termed 'pralaya'.

Each of the planetary stages has seven evolutionary epochs. After the first stage, the 'Saturn stage', came a pralaya followed by the 'Sun stage' which involved a condensation and shrinking in size. We must not confuse this with our present sun although, like all the planets, its substance was already contained within the Sun stage but not yet differentiated or separated out.

Twelve spiritual beings were mainly involved in this evolutionary activity during which even then they put their personal stamp on each phase. Their influence came to be depicted in art and culture as the zodiac which still today influences everything that is alive in evolution. Essentially there are four Cherubim each of whom is accompanied on the right and on the left by another being. Thus there are twelve powers of the Cherubim around the sun who carry out their tasks in this way. This is the original meaning of the zodiac and its symbols. The Cherubim were already present in the Saturn stage, but their influence only became noticeable in the overall evolution during the Sun stage.

The Sun stage, too, underwent seven evolutionary epochs towards the end of which a shining gaseous shape had arisen which corresponded in size to the present-day orbit of Jupiter. The spiritual forces contained and developed within this condensed towards its edges to become a planet, Jupiter.

During the Sun stage of planetary evolution the beginnings of the human physical body were joined by the early beginnings of the ether or life body. In the course of the seven epochs of this stage the system pushed out the animal astrality that belongs to the evolutionary phase of the fishes. These were the archetypal forms of the reptiles, amphibians, lizard fish and dinosaurs and, in a slightly different evolutionary direction, also of the birds.

Gradually the animal astrality was expelled from the whole community of beings. The process may be compared with various different dyes mixed in a liquid being removed one by one until only the clear original fluid remains. The human being was human from the beginning, not an ape or any other animal. The process leading to perfection involved removing from itself step by step the whole of the animal kingdom in its archetypal astral form. Looking at the animal world today we therefore have to say: I once bore those creatures within me as a part of myself; for the sake of my higher development I expelled them from my being.

That remarkable planetary stage also reached the end of its developmental cycle and then disappeared from physical sight in a pralaya. The third planetary stage of our solar system is now termed 'Old Moon'. This contained within itself only the undifferentiated substances of our present moon. The labours of the Kyriotetes or Spirits of Wisdom led to its form by means of further compression and reduction in size. The cosmic dimension of its final phase corresponded roughly with the present orbit of Mars, and the present planet Mars remains as the physical substrate of its existence.

During this third systemic metamorphosis the human being developed a third principle of his being, the astral body. This was and still is directly influenced by the Archai, the Spirits of Personality; and it is the Archangeloi or Spirits of Fire who influence the ether body. The Archai give the human being the character of a personality able to experience joy, pain and all the other attributes. Through the Archangeloi he receives the forces of growth and healing and also all the types of function within his organism.

Animals at that time possessed only the physical and etheric principles and could therefore neither feel pain nor develop any kind of individual characteristics. Although they were not plants they were at the level of the plants.

Having remained behind in their development during the Sun stage, the animals only took the first step during the subsequent Moon stage where they incorporated their ether body. At that point, in accordance with the plan, human beings had already developed their astral body, which the animals were only able to form and incorporate during the Earth stage.

Thus what is now the greater part of the animal kingdom received its archetypal form during the Sun stage by becoming separated off from the line of human evolution. The present shapes of animal bodies developed gradually under influences that spiritual forces, not all of which were in keeping with evolution, exercised on their group souls. By comparison with the racial differences in human beings, there is a far greater variety in the animal kingdom. These many forms were developed from their seven planetary dwellings by the work of the Dynamis (Spirits of Movement), who were then the leading beings. Initially they formed seven main groups of animals. Later the zodiac constellations also began to exert their influence, so that the changing positions relative to the planetary dwellings of the Spirits of Movement brought forth a multiplicity of animal forms at a time when human beings were not yet physically present on the earth.

So in accordance with their evolution the animals manifested physically on the earth while human beings were still living in the spiritual heights. Today, like human beings, they have their physical, ether and astral body in the physical world, while their group-'I' works on them from the astral plane giving them guidance and life. Human beings, on the other hand, have now taken their spiritual 'I' into themselves and have thus become individuals.

Where religious or cultural ideas still retain some knowledge of world evolution people maintain a loving and friendly relationship with the animals. But the materialistic concepts about creation prevalent in the West mean that on the whole animals are met with an unfeeling lack of understanding. Here both philosophy and science hold to the view also 'confirmed' by Church circles that animals have no soul. Combined with the Darwinist theory of evolution and with forgetfulness about the real evolution of the earth, such ideas have led to many untenable interpretations of phenomena in the animal and human kingdoms, for example the 'retrograde evolution' supposedly seen today in sightless animals. These animals are the descendants of animal forms that separated off from humans at a time when Sun and Earth were still united, so in fact these creatures never had eyes. Only once Sun and Earth had separated during the first third of the Moon stage of evolution did sunlight come into being, but before that they neither needed eyes nor could they develop them. The rare cave-dwellers of our time have never possessed eyes throughout the whole length of their evolution.

The third of the seven evolutionary stages of our planetary system and our earth, the stage of 'Old Moon', has some peculiarities that should be mentioned.

After about one third of Old Moon's physical existence, another planetary body split off from it—a proper moon. The remaining larger part then developed into a proper sun, what we would today call a fixed star. This moon circled around its sun until both of them reunited towards the end of the Old Moon period and then disappeared temporarily from physical view in another pralaya. A process of division such as this does not always happen without a struggle, especially when some heavenly beings who have become retarded in their development are involved. Both these circumstances played a part in this first planetary split, and this gave rise not only to the larger planetary bodies but also to countless small and very small asteroids which at that time found their orbits in the space between the orbits of Jupiter and Mars and have come to be known as the asteroid ring. The fact that the Dynamis, the Spirits of Movement, had attained to varying levels of development and maturity played a part in causing this event.

All forms of evolution and spiritual being—regardless of

physical shape, size or level of development—are subject to a cosmic law that comes into play when there are varying degrees of development within a spiritual community. The resulting event plays an important part in the process of our evolution. When individual forms evolve at two different speeds within a community of spirits, this prevents either group from attaining the evolutionary conditions it needs. For a while they therefore part, completely in physical terms and spiritually almost completely, whereby one group advances while the other is retarded in the same measure. The former bond remains during this period. This becomes a cosmic obligation or promise whereby, having developed greater spiritual faculties, the group that can continue to advance owing to the sacrifice made by the other is obliged in turn to assist the lower group in its evolution.

This process took place between human beings on Old Moon who were developing at different speeds, leading at that time to the first parting of humans from the so-called 'sun beings'. The latter therefore felt responsible for their former brothers and assisted them in their turn. Later the same cosmic law was the basis for a necessary split between human beings and animals. Our own still valid cosmic promise to assist our fellow creatures who have remained at a lower stage stems from this split.

In human beings the divine, cosmic evolutionary impulses of love and wisdom are present in different ways in each principle of their being, and they will be developed further. The union between wisdom and love which we must work to acquire on our own planet will lead to the creation of morality.

This is not so in the case of the animals. Here the impulse of love exists at an elementary level and only physically as the love between partners or between parents and offspring while they are still children. The spiritual beings of the animals are scarcely aware of love, having so far developed only wisdom to a higher degree. So the obligation on human beings arising from their separation from animals consists in helping them to comprehend the divine impulse of all-encompassing love. When they die, individual animals mediate to the group soul their experiences with human beings on this score.

Those who strive to prevent cruelty to animals and commit themselves to working for our fellow creatures may be experiencing an unconscious memory of this obligation, and the emotion they feel stems from a justifiable indignation when the promise is not honoured.

When the sun departed during the third—the Old Moon—planetary stage, it took with it highly differentiated spiritual substances. In accordance with the laws of the cosmos, this caused all the remaining kingdoms—the human, animal and plant kingdoms—to be downgraded. (There was as yet no mineral kingdom.) In consequence, the human beings of that time reverted to an evolutionary level somewhere between today's human and animal kingdoms. The animals went to a level somewhere between today's animal and plant kingdoms, and correspondingly the plant kingdom became a kind of 'plant-mineral'. A 'human-animal' came into being that was higher than today's most advanced animals but not yet a human being in the present or cosmic sense. Furthermore an 'animal-plant' evolved and, as already mentioned, a 'plant-mineral'. This remained as the status quo until the end of that planetary stage when sun and moon were reunited and the whole then disappeared into a pralaya.

The subsequent fourth, and present, planetary stage of our solar system is termed 'Earth' in esoteric parlance. This is not yet our present planet earth as we know it, but a system. In cosmological terminology, a stage of evolution is always named after the planetary body that plays an important part in it.

When the Earth stage became physical, once again following the cosmic law we have mentioned, the 'human-animal' kingdom divided into two groups. The lower group became our present animals so that the higher group could ascend to the human phase. In a parallel process the 'animal-plant' kingdom divided in order to contribute to the creation of our present animal and plant kingdoms, and similarly the 'plant-mineral' kingdom also divided, contributing to the additional creation of the mineral kingdom. Thus our present four kingdoms of nature arose during the transition from the third to the fourth planetary stage of evolution.

We should not imagine that the human being was ever an animal like those now present on our earth, not even a higher animal. Animal bodies are incapable of sustaining a human 'I', so they have remained at the group stage in their evolution.

It is the present evolutionary task of human beings to take in and sustain the 'I' as the directing principle of the other three principles of our make-up. By taking in the 'I' we also take on responsibility for the evolution of the Earth, and this calls for knowledge about the cosmic laws.

There were, however, a small number of beings who had advanced further but were too weak to develop or sustain the 'I'. In accordance with the evolutionary law they had to regress to the animal state and thus became what we now know as the anthropoid apes.

Having passed through a pralaya, every newly arising planetary stage has to undergo a brief recapitulation of all the physical states of the previous evolutionary forms of the solar system. This means that the Earth had to pass much more briefly than before through the developmental conditions of Saturn, Sun and Old Moon. For the present cycle of our earth these are termed the Polarean, Hyperborean and Lemurian periods, and their physical forms and consistency corresponded to the prior forms of the planet's incarnations: a body of warmth, a body of air and light, and a body of water.

With regard to the evolution of humanity and the animal kingdom the Lemurian period is especially significant because the physical and spiritual differences caused the split into sun and moon, i.e. fixed star and planet, to be repeated. The subsequent conditions also had to become further differentiated. During the first third a division between sun and earth therefore took place again, and this brought our present planets into existence. At that point the earth still had the present moon within it, while the sun at first contained the other planets. The asteroids also came into being once more.

Later, however, some of the 'sun spirits' who had departed had to undergo a retrograde evolutionary step similar to that of our anthropoid apes. This took place in another dimension, on another level, and necessitated the formation of their own planetary bodies. A small group of the beings who had departed with the sun did not find there the substance base they needed for their own evolution because it was too delicate and subtle. So two lower, although compared with ours higher, planets were divided off together with the inhabitants that belonged to them and became Venus and Mercury. This circumstance is especially interesting for us because most of the teachers who brought us their wisdom in various ways during and also after the Lemurian period came from there. These beings of the highest development, for example the

Buddha, were not the only ones to influence our earth, however, for the fallen leading spirit of the Venus planet of that time, Lucifer, also came. Owing to his excessive pride in his spiritual brilliance, his exaggerated self-confidence not tempered by love and his denial of the Cosmic Word, he underwent a steady decline and today exerts influence on people's astrality.

Having divided off from the sun, the earth which still contained the moon underwent a severe evolutionary deterioration that caused it to become barren and almost mummified to a degree that made it virtually uninhabitable both physically and spiritually. It was hardly possible for human beings to incarnate there, for their 'I' was barely able to influence their physical body. The creatures of the other kingdoms of nature also found no life-sustaining regions and were thus prevented from evolving further. They died out and the earth became almost uninhabitable. Only a few isolated human beings were left on the earth to prevent its form of cosmic evolution from being extinguished. Most human souls found dwellings and evolutionary possibilities on other planets.

To enable the earth to fulfil its set task once again and provide a proper basis for the planned creation and evolution of the four kingdoms, it became necessary for the forces and substances which were preventing evolution to be removed. The leading Sun Beings, the Elohim (Spirits of Form) therefore decided to separate the moon off from the earth in accordance with the laws of the cosmos. This took place during the second half of the Lemurian period. Only by being separated off in this way and relieved of its burden could the earth gradually become habitable again and provide an evolutionary base for all four kingdoms of nature. This new beginning also became our genesis, with the separation of earth and moon leading not only to the birth of humanity but also to its separation into two sexes represented by Adam and Eve.

Only very gradually did the earth regain its ability to sustain its denizens spiritually, physically and with its forces of life. The kingdoms of nature developed at different speeds owing to the different evolutionary directions they had followed. First came the mineral kingdom, then the plant kingdom and after that the animal kingdom. Much later humanity also returned in its present physical guise.

The description of the population, or rather repopulation of the earth giving Adam and Eve as the first human beings is correct in its depiction of the sequence of the four kingdoms of nature. As far as their appearance in material form is concerned, this ties in with present-day science. But it reverses the actual sequence of events. Only in the Book of Revelation, if we can read it aright, do we find the actual evolutionary and temporal sequence described correctly.

Humanity did indeed first appear in its present physical manifestation during the Lemurian period, and this makes modern ethnological and biblical interpretations of the genesis of humanity and of the earth comprehensible. But this explanation cannot claim unqualified accuracy as a description of cosmic laws and the overall evolution of humanity.

We could take the following statement by Rudolf Steiner as our motto for the way we study the evolution of the earth and its inhabitants: 'Information and communications about cosmic truths are so important because morality and ethics cannot be preached. They only develop in equal measure with our knowledge of the spiritual laws of creation and cosmic interrelatedness.'

Looking towards the coming fifth evolutionary stage of our earth, the Jupiter stage, Steiner also expressed his observations about the general principle of evolution: 'It is a cosmic law which applies unceasingly everywhere that evolution causes units to divide into dualities before later reuniting in accordance with karmic laws to form a unit once again.' Humanity will gradually be hampered in its evolution by the circumstance that it possesses the makings both of good and evil, of beauty and ugliness, of truth and lies. Long ago it astrally expelled similarly hampering characteristics in the form of animals. In future its spiritual evolution will require these other hampering characteristics to be split off as well.

Humanity will continue to advance, and in the next evolutionary stage of the earth, the Jupiter stage, it will expel a new kingdom of nature. This kingdom will not have animal forms but will have the appearance of human beings.

A race of humans will arise that embodies the human passions which evolution requires shall be separated off. They will carry that part of evil which people today still bear within themselves and can therefore hide. Once this has happened, it will no longer be possible for those passions to be hidden because they will be clearly recognizable in the physiognomy of that interim race. So in addition to the three lower kingdoms of nature there will be two human kingdoms on the earth. These will be similarly separated from one another in their lifestyle and habitation as are the other kingdoms.

The superiority and corresponding obligation towards the animals as their carers and leaders which creation has enjoined upon human beings has been displaced by arrogance, and the responsibility once taken on has been forgotten. For thousands of years humans have been inconsiderately using, misusing and exploiting animals for their own purposes. Threadbare excuses are used to justify every imaginable form of exploitation, torture and disfigurement, including robbing them of their freedom to evolve.

For us pain is necessary so that we can gain experience about how to adapt to the continuing divine ordering that governs our evolution. But the pain inflicted on animals throughout the whole animal kingdom for profit and out of egoism is not necessary. The present-day excesses of this misuse of animals 'in the service of science' is what is known as vivisection.

Not one of the many anti-vivisectionist efforts that have been set in train has been able to halt the constantly rising methodical, supposedly scientific, sanctioned cruelty to animals because the commercial interests and individual egoism backing it are too strong. Troubled consciences are targeted by half-true arguments while the real circumstances are suppressed. The impression is that all too often these are gratefully accepted because they make people feel exonerated and excused.

Surely we must feel it to be unjust that animals, which cannot look forward to another incarnation, are made to suffer so much and are sent to their death fully conscious. Esoteric research has given us insight into the unalterable justice of the divine creation as it affects the one who causes suffering and the one who suffers. Whether we cause suffering, pain or torture to animals on purpose or by mistake, whether we merely tolerate it or take an active part, whether we cite science as our reason or invoke the law or some other abstract higher authority, we shall in every case be confronted with it again during the period we spend in kamaloca after death. (Rudolf Steiner.) Whether we have done it by mistake or because of medical necessity or for any other 'good reason', this will not be sufficient to justify let alone legitimize such an action. The law of the spiritual life is unbending.

When the individual concerned arrives on his journey after death at the place in time when he caused pain to another living creature he has to suffer the same torture and anguish even more painfully. In his own soul he has to go through what other creatures have suffered by his actions. So the kamaloca of a vivisectionist is especially terrible. In a future life the painful consequences of his activities will remain with him in his subconscious. So a human soul will never again become involved in vivisection or any other torture of living creatures. The ineradicable memory will prevent him from repeating such actions.

Justice is also done to the animals involved. Spiritual science tells us that there will be future consequences following all the torture and deaths inflicted on animals. When human beings interfere in the evolution and integrity of animals in ways that damage their development, every pain and death will return and rise up again in balance, though not via the path of reincarnation. The animal will not return in its original form; what will return will be its soul, which experienced the suffering. In the next developmental stage of the earth the animal soul will be allotted the opposite feeling in equal measure. This will happen because its negative feelings will be recreated by parasitic animals that will reincarnate and inhabit the human being. Out of the circumstances and feelings that evolve in this way will arise the cosmic compensation for the pain it has suffered.

This is the unvarnished esoteric truth, though it may be unpalatable for us today. Even in our present life something similar is already taking place, slowly and gradually. Why are people today plagued by creatures such as bacteria and viruses, which according to cosmic criteria are neither animals nor plants? Such manifestations and their destiny have been brought into life by suffering caused to our fellow creatures in former incarnations. The justice of creation cannot permit one creature to be harmed by another without a corresponding compensation.

The further development of animals that will take place in accordance with the laws of evolution will lead to the group souls of the animals undergoing the same experiences as are undergone by human beings today. In future they will be single individuals with an individual body and an individual soul, although they will never be human beings as we know them. From the group souls will develop beings of the same kind as humans but in another form. The stage of being human can be gone through in different ways, as was the case with the beings from the Saturn, Sun and Moon stages of the earth who preceded us.

Certainly, though, these beings remember their evolutionary duties towards their 'fellow creatures', for if they did not we would not have received or still be receiving from them the help they have always given us.

10
The Cosmic Evolution of Spiritual and Human Beings

In order to evolve, humanity has a constant need for spiritual truths about the cosmos, which are, however, not entirely comprehensible at all times. Everything human beings are able to fathom regarding their development, everything they are able to learn and know, all the concepts and ideas they are able to acquire—all such experiences come to them from elsewhere. They cannot know anything that has not already been experienced, thought through and known in advance by divine individualities who are their superiors in rank. So human thinking is a cognition or re-cognition of circumstances and events that have taken place in the spiritual worlds.

In the Atlantean period, which followed on from Lemurian times, human beings had a clear view of the creative powers at work behind everything material while being able to see the physical world only dimly. The early Atlanteans would have been as little able to perceive what we see with our eyes today as we are now capable of perceiving the spiritual worlds. In those times the planets, too, were not seen as we see them now. Rather there was a kind of sensing perception of all the exertions of the hierarchical beings living on them for whom, as remains the case today, the planetary bodies provided a physical base. What human beings saw were the leading spiritual beings of the cosmos, and what they felt was their influence in their own planets. This continued in ever-decreasing intensity right into the first half of post-Atlantean times. An important change set in around 3000 years before the Christian era when the Kali Yuga began.

As recently as ancient Greek times people did not mean the physical planet when they spoke of, for example, Mercury but rather the totality of all the beings dwelling there. In all the various languages the words Moon, Mercury, Venus, Sun, Mars, Jupiter and Saturn were used to designate the hierarchy of their spiritual inhabitants, whereas today they refer only to the smallest perceivable part within their gigantic etheric and astral fields of force, namely, the physical planet. People knew in those days that a planet's spiritual and etheric fields of force were pretty much identical with the dimension of its orbit. It is this different view of the matter that is the cause of today's irreconcilable contradictions between the earlier Ptolemaic and the subsequent medieval Copernican views of the solar system. The former quite rightly considered the earth to be the spiritual centre of the system, whereas today it is the physical sun that is defined as the astronomical centre while the spiritual dimension is no longer a part of the picture.

Throughout human evolution this was known in all the Mystery schools and by every high priest of former religions, so it was not considered to be a matter of incompatible views. Dionysius the Areopagite, for example, the apostle Paul's most intimate pupil in Athens, repeatedly related that in the space of our solar system, and indeed in the whole of the cosmos, there were not only physical planetary bodies but also spiritual forces and beings superior to humans. He set great store by this distinction and therefore used spiritual names for the planetary sequence: Angeloi, Archangeloi, Archai; Exusiai, Dynamis, Kyriotetes; Thrones, Cherubim, Seraphim.

Above the earth's four visible kingdoms of nature there exists the invisible kingdom of the Angeloi, Archangeloi and Archai. Each group respectively underwent its own human phase of development on one of the previous planetary stages of the Earth: the Archai on Old Saturn, the Archangeloi on Old Sun, and the Angeloi on Old Moon. Of course it goes without saying that the external conditions and also the human form and bodily consistency were different in each case. The Angeloi have now reached the stage which present human beings will have reached when the Earth stage as a whole will have moved on to the next, the Jupiter stage.

For the purpose of preserving the experiences and accumulated knowledge of every individual human being so that when born anew on the earth each can build on these in following the course of a present life, each of us has an angel, usually called our guardian angel. He stands on guard with perpetual awareness from one incarnation to the next, and if we approach the matter in the right way we can to some extent tap into his knowledge.

For the whole duration of a life the angel is bound to aid and guide the human being for whom he is responsible, and this means that in turn the individual human being, in addition to the obligation to undergo his own development, shares in the consequences for his guardian spirit that arise out of the way he behaves during that lifetime.

The next higher level of the hierarchies, the Archangeloi or archangels, are not concerned with individual humans but have the more far-reaching task of guiding larger groupings such as whole nations. They help individuals relate in a positive and harmonious way to their national group and to what may be termed the folk-soul that regulates the relationship between individuals and their nation's totality. The folk-soul is an individual spirit of considerable stature who exerts great influence on everything, including the human beings, within his sphere of influence.

The Archai or Spirits of Personality, who are the next in the hierarchy, carry out an even higher task in connection with humanity. Each according to its own innate being regulates the conditions faced by humanity as a whole by changing the times in sequence, so that in every new incarnation people all over the world meet and experience changed and new evolutionary conditions. The concept of a cultural epoch or time-spirit is a spiritual reality of great importance and decisive effect.

The time-spirit of an epoch encompasses more or less every nation. He brings about the attitude of soul or consciousness of individual humans within a cultural epoch. In keeping with the plan of evolution he arranges for individual human beings with special knowledge and powers to be present in his specific epoch so that the necessary wisdom can come into effect properly. It is the time-spirit who sees to it that specific individuals are present who have precisely defined earthly tasks to carry out.

The Archai entrust a part of their work, the creation of the specific character of a time period, to a select group of Archangeloi whose task it becomes to herald their plans. Long ago in the 'brilliant light' of Old Sun they proclaimed the previous stage of the warmed-through Old Saturn. Similarly in rotating sequence they continue to carry out the orders of the Archai and mediate their impulses into form. 'Angelos' means 'messenger', so as messengers of the Archai they came to be named Archai-Angeloi or Archangeloi. Over a period of 307 years each takes a turn in being responsible for and inspiring a cultural epoch for which in sequence they use the cosmic forces of a specific planet. The sequence of their activities is known from religious sources:

Michael	Sun	Eternal Progress
Oriphiel	Saturn	Cosmic Memory
Anael	Venus	Fulfilment in Love
Zachariel	Jupiter	Cosmic Wisdom
Raphael	Mercury	Liberation of Souls
Samael	Mars	Cosmic Word
Gabriel	Moon	Creation of Form

In Genesis the Archai acting as time-spirits are named 'yom' which means 'day'. In the Egypto-Chaldean cultural epoch before decadence set in they were the beings who were contacted by the priests who had been initiated by the hierophants. During the epoch of ancient India they inspired the seven Holy Rishis and formulated their pronouncements. And by now they have fully absorbed the Christ Impulse.

Some of these Spirits of Personality did not fulfil their development on Old Saturn in the proper way. These retarded beings created out of themselves each animal group-'I' which became ancestors of our present-day kingdom of both the cold and warm-blooded animals.

The tasks of the three groups of the third hierarchy, the Archai, Archangeloi and Angeloi, are thus predominantly concerned with human evolution on the earth and could therefore also be described by a modern term as being 'planet specific'.

The three groups of the second hierarchy, the Exusiai or Spirits of Form, the Dynamis or Spirits of Movement, and the Kyriotetes or Spirits of Wisdom, have tasks that range far beyond the earth and reach into the interplanetary region. This is where the cosmic links among the planets of our system are regulated and coordinated. Beings are needed who will watch over the development conditions of planets until the end of human evolution and also over the transition of human beings and the planet through a pralaya. These beings are the Exusiai, the lowest level of the second hierarchy.

Until about 3000 years before Christ, human beings perceived the stellar beings and the dimension in which they existed in a way that resembled our own seeing today. Thereafter, spiritual seeing waned while physical seeing increased. When this process of change lasting many centuries was completed the etheric and astral forces were no longer perceptible.

The Ptolemaic world view with the earth at its centre remains the view in the sphere of the hierarchical beings, and our present planets continue to mark its various boundaries.

With the earth as the metaphysical centre of the system, the sphere of influence of the Angeloi reaches to the moon, that of the Archangeloi to Mercury and that of the Archai to Venus. The Exusiai dominate and influence the space up to the sun and the Dynamis more or less up to the orbit of Mars. The sphere of the Kyriotetes reaches up to Jupiter and that of the Thrones to Saturn. These are the understandable consequences of their various evolutionary activities, among which the Thrones gave the substance through which Saturn could evolve.

The most important aspect of the way these structures are arranged is that all the etheric and astral force fields overlap and converge in the centre, our earth. So the inhabitants of our planet are exposed to the influences of all the hierarchical levels.

Originally all the planetary bodies were contained within the sun, and even once the sun had split off they remained within its immediate sphere of influence. In this way, since it is the seat of the highest hierarchical beings, the Elohim, it is the main directing 'planetary' body of our system. The Elohim's most lofty leader is Christ who right from the beginning of our evolution has had the task of guiding humanity and who will retain this office in varying ways until it is completed.

Students of astrology will also be interested in an important point concerning the planets Venus and Mercury which is noticeable when old and newer stellar charts are compared. Present nomenclature nominates Mercury as being the planet closest to the sun, followed by Venus. The reverse was once the case, as is obvious in the older charts.

Science also regards the old Ptolemaic world system as being outdated and no longer relevant. This will change, however, when people become able once more to perceive and assess the more spiritual aspects of the cosmos.

Since the most ancient times the helping beings of the hierarchies in the cosmos have been effective on the earth in very many different ways. The sons of Venus and Mercury, especially, have been in contact with us frequently since Lemurian times. The Venus beings saw it as their task to transmit cosmic wisdom, so that under their influence, among other developments, various religions and cults came into being. The sons of Mercury were as powerful as present-day folk-spirits and were more concerned with guiding groups of human beings. Both therefore played important parts in the evolution of human beings on earth. The Bodhisattvas belong among them.

In those ancient times and still today such individuals look no different from any others. Only a clairvoyant can tell the difference at the etheric and astral level. The spirit of such an individual reaches as far as the region of Mercury or Venus and possesses the cosmic wisdom of those planetary intelligences. Although limited to a physical body, the guiding spiritual power of such beings as well as their influence on the whole of humanity is immense.

After the Saturn stage of evolution the air and light body of the Sun stage began to develop. When this happened, the Seraphim, Cherubim and Thrones began to differentiate and build up this substance outside it in keeping with creation. If a human individual with the necessary wisdom had then existed within that body, he would have been able to sense those forces coming from various directions and would have been able to indicate the direction of the cosmos from which they came most strongly and also point out the destiny towards which they tended. By pointing to the specific constellation it would have been possible to determine and record the exact direction. In this way the forces were perceived and utilized by the Exusiai, Dynamis and Kyriotetes working on the human being within that heavenly body.

The archetypal physical form of the human being was laid down in keeping with the warmth substance of the Saturn stage. The first to be created were the beginnings of the heart. Its origin can be traced back to a movement stimulus within the warmth substance. Ancient mystics saw this as being connected with forces emanating from the constellation of Leo. Very gradually fundamental connections evolved between the parts of our body and the influences emanating from the cosmos. Ancient Mystery wisdom tells us that all the parts of our body are connected with specific signs of the zodiac and continue to be influenced by them throughout life.

The human torso is encased in a kind of 'breastplate', the bony thorax, and this is what it is called in the ancient books of the Chaldeans. To symbolize this an animal was chosen that was clothed in similar body-armour, the crab (Cancer).

The origins of a symmetrical structure of the body arose under the influence of Gemini and those of the upper part of the head under that of the ram (Aries). Aquarius, the water carrier, influenced the origin of the legs and Pisces, the fishes, that of the feet.

In the Mystery teachings of the Old Testament the cosmic formative forces of the Seraphim and Cherubim are given the name of 'Adam Cadmon'. Such teachings will one day reappear in the wisdom knowledge of humanity.

Behind what people today call material substance there lie a great multiplicity of forces and influences. Some well-known physicists have indeed begun to remark that physical matter as it is now defined cannot actually exist and that in fact the 'form' we perceive is nothing other than a con-centrated field of forces. This is surely a welcome step towards a realization of reality.

Working together in complex ways with other influences, the forces of the Spirits of Form and the Spirits of Move-ment create all the manifestations of what we call animate and inanimate nature. The total human and animal body as well as all the different organs in both of these come into being in this way. For the most part the first hierarchy is responsible for the human being and the second hierarchy for the animal.

The beings of the hierarchies relate in different ways to the divine sphere of the Trinity. Only the Seraphim, Cherubim and Thrones have direct sight of the Godhead, and every-thing they do God does through them. Human beings will have to work towards and seek such direct sight throughout their long evolution.

As members of the second group of three, the Spirits of Wisdom, Movement and Form do not have a direct sight of God but only of his manifestations. Their direct impulse is to comply with these.

For human beings to have the choice between following an evolution towards God or developing a different kind of attitude, a possibility of choice first had to be created. For this reason some beings of the Dynamis group were detailed off to strengthen human beings in their development towards the highest goal by placing obstacles in their path. These 'gods of hindrance' were never evil in themselves. They were necessary and tolerated promoters of evolution through the possibility they created for behaviour that could run counter to the purpose of creation. As knowledge of the reasons for their existence waned they of course gradually came to be classed as 'evil'. All the Mysteries describe this procedure as a 'war in the heavens'.

The first beings to be confronted with this possibility to decide in favour of one direction or another were the Angeloi who stand in rank directly above us. This happened during the Moon stage of evolution. Since one part decided to follow these temptations they split into two groups. One continued on the path of evolution planned by the divine. The other at first joined forces with impulses of opposition and later, in the Lemurian age, with the astral being of man while his physical body was coming into existence and shortly before he received his divine 'I'. This procedure is generally termed the 'fall of man'.

The 'fallen angels' are known as the beings of Lucifer and he is their leader. The result for human beings is that they enjoy the freedom of choice: they can either enter into error, lies and evil or they can rise above these through their own efforts and emerge strengthened from the attacks.

These luciferic influences are due to remain in the world for long ages to come and they will make their mark on all individuals. Only moral strength and behaviour towards the world around them will enable them to resist.

Another influence that does not conform to creation came into existence through the being called Ahriman. The ahrimanic powers strive to deaden human beings' awareness of their spiritual origins. Ahriman wants to persuade them that they are nothing more than rather perfectly developed animals. His ideas fit very well with today's scientific attitudes. All he wants us to know about is the sense-perceptible and tangible world that our present biological make-up enables us to perceive.

Human beings are thus positioned between these two opposing forces. And their planned path of development requires them to reach and hold a balance between them. The result is actually a trinity: Lucifer—Human Being—Ahriman. Earlier initiates often pointed to this circumstance, whereby the tendency of the luciferic powers was to be controlled and comprehended for the purpose of unfolding spiritual freedom and the ahrimanic forces were to be applied to comprehending and grasping reality.

It is understandable that knowledge of such things is meant to be prevented or become confused. One of the steps undertaken in this direction was to replace the effectiveness of the trinity of active forces by a duality of antagonistic forces. This applies to all tendencies to simplify matters by setting up contrasting pairs like good and evil, God and the devil, or even heaven and hell. It is almost impossible to foresee the extent and influence of such a 'rearrangement'. It began during the Eighth Ecumenical Council of the year 869 in Constantinople when the hitherto consciously sensed trichotomy of the human being consisting of body, soul and spirit, which had been valid until then, was suddenly declared to be heretical. Theologians and philosophers of the time had great difficulty in rearranging their doctrines to describe the human being as consisting of no more than a body and a soul. Our present ideas hark back to that ruling which later also brought about the schism between the western and eastern Roman Catholic Churches.

As a point of clarification we should mention that Lucifer works in the human being's astral body and Ahriman in the etheric. When the existence of the human spirit is denied it becomes impossible to achieve a balance between them by means of the spirit, the 'I'. The Christ Impulse, too, is only comprehensible when it is seen as a force of balance between Ahriman and Lucifer.

11
Spiritual and Physical Differences Between Humans and Animals

From birth to death the human being's ether body or body of formative forces works to maintain the shape and function of his physical organism, bringing order into all the various mineral substances within it and preventing them from going their own way, which they are only free to do once the physical body dissolves after death.

Beings of the higher hierarchies form the ether body and are the source of its life. A physical body cannot on its own build up and maintain its form by using the substances it contains. Similarly the ether body, too, cannot develop its forces from within itself. It needs the help of a yet more subtle organizing principle, the astral body, which is named after the stars because it maintains contact with the astral world, mostly while the human being is asleep. Human beings received their astral body at the time of Old Moon through sacrifices made by the Dynamis, the Spirits of Movement, and with the help of the Angeloi. It is the bearer of the passions, desires and urges, and especially of egoism. It functions through being linked with the nervous system.

The astral body is also that part of the human being which feels pain. This third principle is possessed by man and in a similar way also by the more developed, warm-blooded animals. In both cases its shape is elliptical and it envelops and extends slightly beyond the physical form.

It also works to allow waking consciousness to come about.

A living being on the earth possessing only an ether body as its highest principle has a consciousness of permanent sleep, like the plants.

Animals are regularly influenced by their environment. They are made aware of the rhythms in their lives by external influences including those of heat and cold, pain and pleasure, and certain repetitive processes such as hunger, thirst, tiredness and the enjoyment of physical activity. In animals emotions and actions are almost always stimulated by processes either inside or outside their body.

For human beings the situation is different because for them life has more to offer than these impressions from inside and outside themselves. They can develop desires, wishes and intentions within themselves that go far beyond the physical or external world. They have interests, ideas and plans the source of which is neither inside nor outside their body but in the fourth principle of their being, their 'I'.

Having been given a sense of identity that is stronger than that of the higher animals they differ from their sisters and brothers in the animal kingdom and have come to be known as the 'lords of creation'. They have the task of gradually developing and reworking the lower principles of their being so that one day they will be able to take sole responsibility for them. As this progresses, the Spirit-self (Manas) will develop from the astral body, the Life-spirit (Buddhi) from the ether body, and the Spirit-man (Atma) from the physical body.

The human body came into being during the time of Old Sun through a sacrifice made by the Kyriotetes, the Spirits of Wisdom. The ether body builds and maintains the whole of the glandular system, regulating it with the direct help of astral and spiritual influences. It also has the important task of operating, regulating and regenerating the formative forces in all the body's organs and tissues. Because there is a species-specific difference in the way the principles of their being work together, the processes of healing and regeneration also differ in humans and animals. In lower animals (and plants) the ether body is not very intimately bound up with the physical body, so it can be fairly independent in the way it works in activating its healing and regenerative forces. That is why damage to the body of a lower animal is relatively easily mended or even a lost limb re-grown. Others achieve this by means of regularly casting off their skin as they grow. In the case of the higher animals and especially human beings the link between astral and ether body is closer and therefore more hampering, so that healing and regeneration are not possible to the same degree.

Other important physiological differences in the etheric sphere arise from the fact that the lower, cold-blooded animals and to a lesser degree also the mammals cannot see objects as clearly as humans despite the fact that anatomically their eyes would make clearer vision possible. Instead they have an additional picture consciousness like that possessed by human beings at the time of Old Moon. So quite apart from what they can perceive optically, the animals experience others etherically through inner pictures that give them either a pleasant or an unpleasant impression. In addition they can sense the intentions of others with their astral body.

These animals do not see objects in as much detail as we do, but they sense whether they are dangerous or not by means of unpleasant or pleasant inner images and can also feel the thoughts and intentions of other creatures astrally. They then respond to the overall impression by dodging, turning away, defending themselves or attacking.

Throughout the whole of life on earth the astral body

remains in contact with the world of the stars. It is responsible for the thinking, feeling and will of a human individual, and also for the ability to be imaginative. A well-balanced form of egoity provides the necessary preliminary stage and foundation for the development of the 'I'.

Being able to bear and sense pain, the astral body is an important instrument in the protection and preservation of the body and its health. The astral principle begins to develop further within the physical body after puberty and is fully active by the twenty-first year of life.

Throughout life it is possible for the organizational principle of the astral body to become spoilt or damaged in various dimensions. The worst means by which this can happen is through immoral behaviour, whereby a weakening of its independence and strength is brought about. That is why the most deep-seated causes of many illnesses can be found at this level. These are usually expressed in weaknesses of the immune system leading to frequent infections.

Human beings are fundamentally different from animals in that their health can be affected by the consequences of several incarnations, but also in that they are able to work at developing the various principles of their being. The astral forces working in them are also different, as are their evolutionary tasks. The human ether and astral bodies work together in a way that is almost antagonistic, which is not the case to the same extent in animals. Animals lack an 'I' as the decisive principle of independence in how they react; this is partially replaced by what we call 'instinct'.

In the lower animals the ether body is unhindered by physical or astral forces in its ability to restore to health or balance every kind of damage to the physical body. In the higher animals the stronger astral body of the species as a whole can be more of an obstacle to the etheric, but never as strongly as is the case in the human being. The forces of healing and regeneration in warm-blooded creatures are weaker than in cold-blooded ones but considerably stronger than in human beings.

Both human beings and warm-blooded animals have the capacity to feel pain, but they differ in that animals are not able to develop themselves further by applying their consciousness to overcoming the pain. So animals suffer more intensely than humans. This is because knowledge and willpower represent a strong counter-current to the sensation of pain which helps to make it relatively more controllable and bearable. Since this possibility does not exist for animals, pain for them is incomparably stronger, more uncomfortable and more all-encompassing.

The way human beings and animals, and indeed the different species of animal, relate to the astral body is exceedingly variable and determined by very different criteria. This is one of the reasons why experimenting on animals to qualify and quantify pain in humans is as useless as is testing pain-relieving substances on them.

Animals do not carry their group-'I' within themselves; they are guided by their group spirit out of the astral realm surrounding the earth by means of what we call instinct. Their astral body is thus the dominant principle in their physical body. They experience the world around them much more intensely and in addition when they need it the entire wisdom of their group soul is at their disposal.

The possibility for humans to take in the 'I' began during the Lemurian period of the Earth stage. Later, during the post-Atlantean period, the being of man was gradually shaped into becoming its bearer. The Spirits of Form endowed human beings with their 'I'. During the Lemurian period some isolated groups began to develop a kind of 'I'-consciousness, but it only really came to be taken in consciously by wider swathes of the population during the time of the Mystery of Golgotha and even later.

The 'I' which came to be directly incorporated into the human being about 2000 years ago was actually the reflection on earth of the spiritual human 'I'. In the physical body the 'I' manifests in the blood which is the bearer of substances essential for life and is also that which maintains all the tasks of the immune system, this being the precondition for an independent organism that is separate from its environment. It organizes the many levels of functional defence against foreign micro-organisms which enter the body by all sorts of routes and which it targets with the help of various blood cells and their functional interchange with various proteins.

Other functions of the 'I' are connected with the personality. Among these are regular and consistent thought processes as well as a logical approach to problems that arise out of observation and interpretation of the perceived environment.

Through their 'I' human beings can also be pleased or displeased by beautiful or ugly, lofty or base, humorous or absurd, harmonious or grotesque impressions. Another expression of the personality is the ability to plan and design actions in advance, to take up a stance with regard to some matter and to formulate a reply.

None of these spiritual or mental achievements is possible for animals whose sensory capacities are considerably more base than the human being's individual awareness. The lack of an 'I' in an animal means that it has very few facial expressions, and rather than laughing or crying it can merely grin or howl.

Animals do have a degree of intelligence and also an instinctive morality which is far more sure and less prone to mistakes than that of human beings. Nevertheless, we cannot attribute to them moral ideas that are on a par with our own. Their individual fate is less important for the group soul as a whole. A single animal is a part of a larger organism, so its behaviour and reactions are governed by other criteria than those of an individual human being.

In their present evolution, another important factor in animals is that their physical appearance is neither brought about by a spiritual individuality, as in the case of humans, nor is it the result of activity on the part of the group soul. Instead the 'fall of man' forced the animals to adopt the forms of the various species. Paul's discussion of this matter in his letter to the Romans may be traced back to a knowledge of such archetypal conditions. It may be regarded as a reminder of the duty human beings have towards the animals:

'Around us creation awaits with great longing the time when the sons of God may be recognized in man. Creation is subject to impermanence for the sake of him who has dragged it down with him into this impermanence. So everything in creation yearns for the future, since the breath of freedom shall also pass through the kingdoms of creation and bring to an end the tyranny of impermanence. In becoming aware of the spirit sphere, creation, too, will pass from unfreedom to the freedom which is the due of all those who have sprung from God.' (Based on Emil Bock's translation into German.)

In former times the various principles of man's being were organized in a different way. The manner in which they relate to one another is expressed throughout the course of a single life between birth and death. Thus by the twenty-eighth year the sentient soul as a part of the personality will have arrived, as will the intellectual soul by the thirty-fifth year and the consciousness soul by the forty-second year. Until this point the workings of the 'I' will have been directed mainly towards establishing the being as a whole, while thereafter the more spiritual further development will proceed in ways not so visible externally.

Tiredness warns us when it is time to do our duty in respect of the day-and-night rhythm. The forces of our intellect that we have used and reduced during the day must be replenished, which happens while we sleep when our 'I' and astral body depart from our physical and ether body in order to enter the spiritual world under the guidance of our guardian angel.

When our 'I' meets with our guardian spirit or genius while our body lies asleep the actions of the day that has passed are assessed and the events of days soon to come are also revealed.

When animals die their physical, etheric and astral existence ends as well. This is even generally the case with the higher animals closest to man. Most of them return to their group soul into which they re-enter having lost their individual sense of being. Their life-experience and the knowledge they have gained in their association with human beings and the other kingdoms of nature are taken up into the wisdom of the group spirit.

Some mature animals which have been closely bound up with a human being cannot or do not wish to find their way back. These set out on a different path of evolution which is open to them as physically invisible nature beings. In most of these cases they become what has been called a 'salamander', which has possibilities of some degree of individualization and also of contact with humans.

This is the evolutionary path embarked on by domesticated, warm-blooded animals which have had an exceptionally close relationship with a human being and have thus developed a strong sense of individuality that makes it difficult for them to return to the group soul. Determined by evolution, some apes and kangaroos, a few amphibians and individualized birds also detach themselves from the animal astrality in order to become nature beings. The animals that have been close to human beings develop into salamanders, while the others become gnomes, nymphs and sylphs. Each then works in its own way in and for nature. In their basic forms and statements, all nature religions fundamentally bear the stamp of this knowledge.

So every connection between humans and animals has consequences that have to be balanced out. Unkind behaviour towards animals causes and activates the creation of correspondingly inimical beings which can act in opposition to people in their next life or even influence other human beings to adopt positions of enmity.

When a human being dies, this does not mean the end of his spiritual 'I' or of his astral principle. Natural death occurs when the forces of the ether and physical bodies have been used up. At the moment of death we experience a brief view of our entire life like a great painting. This comes about as the links between the ether and physical bodies loosen, so that clairvoyance is regained. Once the separation is completed the picture of life disappears.

During the course of this transition into the spiritual world the human being releases elemental beings that he has absorbed during his life on earth. Thus freed, they may return to their original element. But it can also happen that when he reincarnates again he has to take them into himself once more.

Someone who has died enters into the period of kamaloca during which he passes in reverse order through the opposite of all his actions and thoughts. Over a period of time lasting about one third in length of the lifetime just past, he experiences in stronger measure all the joy and all the suffering he has caused to others. This time in kamaloca is the precondition necessary for being able to work with the guiding divine beings at preparing his next life on earth. Death and reincarnation are not a punishment; they are evolution and grace on the way to finding the right way back to the divine, spiritual world.

Much has only been hinted at in the above, for example in regard to the gnomes, undines, sylphs and salamanders. Unlike animals and plants, these earth, water, air and fire beings cannot be seen by human eyes, so that an important part of nature remains imperceptible to us.

In addition to other tasks the gnomes, for example, form the spiritual realm of all the lower animals up to the fishes. They might be described as the intellectual complement of the creatures that need support and protection in this form. Then there are the undines. One of their functions is to shape and create the scales, armour and shells needed by other creatures. The sylphs, meanwhile, help to organize in a similar way everything needed by the birds for which they also maintain necessary links with the earth. And the countless forms of butterflies and other higher insects are cared for and protected by the salamanders who give them whatever help they need in their natural habitat.

Sickness suffered by animals is not caused by karmic debt as is the case with humans. Their illnesses are brought about by the egoistic behaviour of humans which includes the careless exploitation of nature leading to changes in biotopes.

Human beings damage and change the environment to such an extent that many animals can no longer find appropriate surroundings or food. The use in agriculture of pesticides and countless other poisons that cast a heavy burden on living creatures, and also of artificial fertilizers, has damaged the natural environment to such an extent that appropriate living conditions are no longer available.

Continuous forced absorption of artificial poisons from the environment, many of which are not excreted but accumulate in the body, brings about an ever-increasing weakening of the animal organism. The resultant collapse of the immune system means that animals contract fatal diseases or infections that would either not be present or would remain under control in a healthy body or suitable biotope. Selective destruction, displacement or thinning of supposedly unimportant plants in efforts by agriculture and forestry to establish monocultures for the purpose of making optimal use of land has led to the destruction of even narrow field borders that contain plants to which animals would instinctively turn for use as medicine when they contract infections or fall ill. Forced to put up with these conditions, many can no longer help themselves when succumbing to illnesses which now often prove fatal.

Only as human beings evolve further spiritually and morally will they in future once again have access to such knowledge. When that time comes, eating will no longer be a lowly occupation or even one that makes us ill. We will once again know that every food also supplies us with spiritual qualities. To say a grace before meals will then be a natural way of helping us digest the food in ways that are in keeping with creation.

Domestic animals also fall ill through being given fodder

that is unsuitable or chemically poisoned. Often they are especially sensitive in their reaction. Their resistance to disease and even their normal life expectancy is impaired by being fed throughout their lives with additives that are as unnecessary as they are harmful. These are medications that promote rapid weight gain and thus increase profits, heart remedies, tranquillizers, growth hormones, antibiotics and so on, many of which are carcinogenic pharmaceutical preparations. All these are administered 'prophylactically' in an uncontrolled way whether there are symptoms of disease or not and without any regard for the quality of the resulting meat. To avoid having to find a cheap outlet or take it to the knacker's yard the stock is quickly slaughtered on the farm and the meat sold off as fit for consumption.

The so-called 'free market economy' evidently provides opportunities for growth-glorifying food-production managers, unscrupulous farmers and vets and also thoughtless traders to treat both animals and humans as means for increasing their profits. Being greedy for profit, the pharmaceutical industry, agriculture and commerce are all conspiring to bring about the greatest deterioration in the quality of meat.

Seen from many different angles we cannot avoid the realization that there are people who will have to bear in their karma the responsibility not only for their own diseases and those of their fellow men but also for all the diseases affecting animals and their environment, and in addition for all the torments suffered by domestic animals.

12
Understanding the Biblical Commandments

In their written form the Ten Commandments are today presented in the style of a law in the same way as a state might promulgate its legal requirements, and they are interpreted as if they had the same aim and effect. The only difference is that they were written down over 3000 years ago with the intention that they should remain valid for a much longer time-span than is customary for laws today.

Owing to the inadequate translations available to us and especially on account of various far-reaching changes added later, the versions of the Decalogue at our disposal today misrepresent its real spiritual message. The following is an attempt at rendering its meaning.

First Commandment: I am the eternally Divine, that which you feel within yourself. I have led you out of the land of Egypt where you were unable to follow me within yourself. Henceforth you shall not raise other gods above me. You shall not acknowledge as higher gods those that appear to you as an image out of heaven or those whose influence comes out of the earth or works between heaven and earth. You shall not worship that which is below the divine within yourself, for I am the Divine which is further evolved. I am that which is eternal within you, which works into your body and thereby into the coming generations. If you acknowledge me within yourself, I will live on as you into the one thousandth generation, and the bodies of your people will thrive!

Second Commandment: You shall not speak about me in

error, for every error concerning the 'I' within you will ruin your body!

Third Commandment: You shall distinguish between workdays and holidays so that your life may become an image of my existence. For that which lives as the 'I' within you laboured for six days to create the world, and on the seventh day it lived within itself. Therefore your doings and the doings of your son and of your daughter, of your servants and of your animals and whoever is also with you shall be directed outwards for six days only; and on the seventh day your gaze shall search for me within yourself!

Fourth Commandment: Continue your work in the sense of your father and your mother so that the property remains your own which they acquired for themselves through the strength which I brought into being within them!

Fifth Commandment: Do not commit murder!

Sixth Commandment: Do not commit adultery!

Seventh Commandment: Do not steal!

Eighth Commandment: Do not degrade your neighbour by speaking untruths about him!

Ninth Commandment: Do not begrudge your neighbour his property!

Tenth Commandment: Do not begrudge your neighbour his wife, nor his servants nor the other creatures that enable him to progress!

When we study this thoroughly and absorb its meaning it becomes evident that Moses was being addressed by the same divine power that had announced to him out of the burning bush: 'I am that I am!'

After a long preparation the people of Israel were chosen to be the first to take in, like a droplet of the spirit, this divine part of God's being to help them prepare for future tasks in the history of humanity which they were destined to carry out.

Having thus far felt themselves to be primarily a part of a group, it was from this point onwards that human beings began to individualize and develop into conscious personalities. Other descriptions in the Old Testament point to the gradual and continuing development of this 'I'-awareness. This also brought about a different kind of thinking, a new attitude to life and responsibility which finally necessitated a new social structure. The Ten Commandments were intended to explain the personal responsibility towards one's fellow human beings that arose when one experienced the Divine Name 'I am that I am' and took into one's soul the individualizing effect it had.

Unlike in former times, it is now difficult for us to see any connection between the spiritual and the material worlds; to us it appears as an abstraction. But when this alteration in man's being was proclaimed and then took place it felt like a burst of unimaginable power that altered not only the human being's own consciousness but also the whole structure of the astral, etheric and physical principles of his being. The proclamation of the Ten Commandments led to a noticeably new and stronger feeling of selfhood involving a change in all the conditions of life, responsibility and attitude including that towards health and sickness. Thenceforth individuals were under the obligation—and they were instructed accordingly—to look with responsibility into their own soul and to question themselves about leading a righteous life. There was a clear understanding that not to take account of this new power of the 'I' would lead to the damage and ultimately the destruction of both body and soul.

In contrast to the Israelites, the peoples all around them at that time still worshipped only those gods who had worked on the lower principles of the human being. Images taken from the mineral kingdom represented gods who had worked on the physical body. Religious images taken from the plant kingdom showed gods who had collaborated on the ether body. And images from the animal kingdom symbolized gods who had helped build the astral body. But that which had transformed the human being into the 'lord of creation', the Divine 'I', could not be shown in the form of an external image.

This is why the first Commandment is intended to show that the highest divine impulse that has begun to work in the human being cannot be symbolized in the customary representational form. Among the other peoples only the initiated priests knew about the great Mystery of the 'I' and about the God who must not be depicted in outer images. The majority of the population were not told about this and could not have understood it anyway. So in public life everything depended on these priest-sages and their knowledge. They endeavoured to maintain the public welfare and health by means of other institutions, instructions and powers. The overall social structure of these peoples was adjusted to receiving health under the guidance of the priests and Mystery centres. So to maintain the health of the people various forms of ritual developed and could be consulted, depending on which beings were worshipped, such as the Egyptian temple sleep or the Aspis cult.

Every image or representation, in whatever form, contains and expresses the spirit, and in this the motivations and thoughts of the one who makes them are all-important. The highest impulses of all, however, the ones that emanate from the place where the 'I' meets the supersensible realm, cannot be depicted in images, so every depiction must of necessity contain lower spiritual impulses which the human artist absorbs and then passes on.

Perhaps it is not necessary to mention that our present lifestyle and our attitude and behaviour towards our fellow human beings, the animals and the environment cannot do justice to the requirement not to value other influences more highly than the divine instruction given in the Command- ments in which we are exhorted to recognize and respect the divine in other living beings.

Moses' people were told that when speaking the name of God they must bear in mind: The one who has entered into me must be recognized in proper fashion. The influence of unfavourable beings not conforming to creation can only be diminished with the help of God's power. Those who are responsible for these pathogenic influences are not difficult to recognize. They are Lucifer and Ahriman and their many lower or fallen helpers.

The third Commandment contains a clear indication that with his 'I' the true human being is a microcosm created by God in six days. That is why on the seventh day human beings should rest, so as to become the image of God and also be like God in their deeds.

The fourth Commandment points out that the 'I' must develop and self-awareness must become personalized before individual property can be acquired leading to a sense of ownership. Prior to this such a thing was not possible and would also not have been comprehensible. It applied only to the highest leaders of the people who still possessed some degree of initiation knowledge. It is further pointed out that the property acquired remains linked to the power of the 'I' and should be passed on from father to son and on to the grandson so that the works can be handed down by the strength of the father for the good of the people.

The fifth Commandment contains a realization that can only be comprehended after deeper study of spiritual science: everything connected with any form of killing, destroying or torturing of another living being weakens the power of the 'I' as an expression of the divine impulse in the human being.

This Commandment also hints that any unegoistic assistance given to a fellow creature to help it prosper or regain its health, or to make its life easier or more bearable, or even to increase its stature in the cosmic ranking, sends divine, spiritual forces for body and soul into the one who does these actions. Killing or misusing a living creature—whether it be animal or man—causes these divine, spiritual forces to be reduced so that the ability to regain health is at least reduced but more often actually damaged. This leads especially in a subsequent incarnation to a disposition towards ill health, to specific illnesses or deficiency in development.

Similar aspects are also expressed in the sixth and seventh Commandments, in which the main meaning and thought content culminates thus: Marriage forms a centre for the strengthening of the powers of the 'I'. The one who breaks his marriage weakens the strength of his individuality because the strength he had gained from his marriage wanes and no longer gives him any inner security. In the same way stealing, and the lying inevitably linked with it, weakens the individuality.

The final Commandments express how a person's lack of an ability to control or direct his desires reduces the spiritual forces streaming within him because egoistic interests in the form of wrong attitudes to life are a major factor in not recognizing and not accepting the divine impulse.

On the astral plane, thoughts filled with passions, desires and untruths form new beings of a type that might be described as artificial elemental beings.

Love on the other hand enhances the power of the 'I'. Resentment, envy or hatred destroy it just as it is destroyed if we degrade the value of our fellow human beings or if we speak untruths about them or hate them. Even desiring or lusting after someone else's possessions brings about a weakening of the 'I', which in turn leads to an impairment of one's resistance to disease. As a result one becomes especially susceptible to infections.

The instructions of the Ten Commandments were given to enable human beings, depending on their level of development, to approach an entirely new age under the influence of the power of their 'I'. They should be seen as a way of preparing humanity to take in the Mystery of Golgotha in which the divine healing power was to come to an even clearer expression in the human individual.

The Romans partially comprehended the deeper spiritual meaning, still valid today though no longer understood in the same way, expressed in the phrase *Nomen est omen*. We would do well to regard the name of Jesus, the Christ-bearer, under the same aspect. In his time he was hailed as 'Jehoshua', which in Hebrew means 'He who heals from within God'.

13
Hidden Aspects of Sickness and Health

Millions of cells die off during every second of a long human life while as many again are newly produced. This amounts to a destruction and renewal rate of hundreds of billions of cells per day. The bone marrow of a healthy adult produces 200 million red blood corpuscles per second.

The total mucous membrane of the small intestine (endo-thelium) has a surface measuring about 600 square metres and it is completely regenerated in one week. The number of cells thus newly formed is beyond anything a normal person can imagine.

Over the course of a single day the body of an adult produces in intermediary metabolism about 70kg of adenosine triphosphoric acid which is immediately used up again in energy processes.

Such figures give a picture of the all-embracing, integrative complexity that is involved in maintaining the precision of these reciprocal and compensatory functions in our human organism. The 12,000 billion individual cells, which are constantly being regenerated, are governed by the 'I' and organized by the etheric and astral principles of our being. Throughout our life we have to combat the tendency of cells to segregate, but we are not always totally successful in this.

If we are to be healthy, all our organs must individually and mutually remain in a creation-related connection with the cosmic forces that maintain them and with the 'I' which is set above them.

To live as spiritual beings according to the will and laws of the Creator and maintain the conditions required for our health we must begin to realize the importance of our existence and of our links with other beings, and also our responsibility towards the whole of creation as well as the sanctity of every physical body. In order to comprehend our evolutionary obligations we must know that we live through many incarnations, and we must understand that forces not compatible with creation can also work in us. Living in a harmonious and balanced way can protect us against these influences. In this sense illnesses are an important educational and developmental factor through which we can learn what we need to understand. They are an essential part in everyone's biography and cannot be avoided or suppressed without drastic consequences. At the latest in our next incarnation, every symptom we suppress without removing its real karmic cause forces our being to shift the illness not properly dealt with on to another level.

This is where we come up against the dangers inherent in current medicine which tries to explain diseases as happening of their own accord, thus branding them as the enemy. Hence the constant talk of fighting disease without endeavouring to recognize its deeper causes. Medical treatises often read like war reports that omit any mention of defeats. After all these victories, why is the enemy still in existence? It appears that scalpel, injections, tablets and radiation make no impression on it. But perhaps this is just as well. If diseases could be conquered by these means there would be no further opportunity for human beings to make any progress in their evolution.

Medicine today regards every illness as unnecessary, accidental and meaningless. In this it fails in its duty to research adequately and make known the connection between disease and lifestyle. Indisposition and illness are the inevitable result of abusing one's body for years or even throughout life with unsuitable eating habits, poor-quality foods and meat, damaging beverages, irregular habits and mental impoverishment, a polluted atmosphere and environment, and immoral influences of all kinds.

In addition society, especially in the West, has placed the professions of physician and medical scientist on an undeserved pedestal of infallibility. Responsible authorities in all past cultures would have rejected present medical attitudes as unsuitable and unspiritual. In our age, however, people accept every statement regardless of its content and for reasons of expediency identify with opinions that are not even seemingly justifiable.

Out of a strange fear of getting involved with something unknown, academic training makes scrupulous efforts to side-step any necessity of linking medicine with spiritual knowledge or religion. If such a link were to be brought about, attitudes would change and crucial transformations in people's understanding of medicine and health would result. Is this perhaps why such ideas are dismissed out of hand?

For millennia in the past, medical care consisted in prophylaxis and the prevention of disease, and the population in general were educated on the basis of this understanding. But now the main emphasis is on diagnosis and therapy, which can of course only begin once an illness has become obvious—by which time it is far more difficult to treat with natural remedies that do not do any further damage. Natural remedies take longer to remove the symptoms and also call for active participation by patients who nowadays are anxious to achieve quick results and therefore prefer fast-acting medication.

If spiritual science were to become the basis on which medical experience could be evaluated, it would be necessary to return to the principle of prophylaxis. Routine check-ups would then home in on a patient's disposition to a particular disease, which could be treated in good time by natural medicines, diet or psychosomatic methods. There is every reason to suppose that such a way forward would be successful, so it should be followed purposefully and linked with appropriate spiritual healing methods as well. Operating theatres with their expensive investment in technology and personnel would for the most part become redundant, as would the productions of the pharmaceutical industry. Sceptics may meanwhile rest assured, however, that at our present level of evolution operating theatres will still be needed for the treatment of accidental injuries, developmental malformations, fractures and every kind of tumour.

As things stand now, medical practitioners declare patients to be healthy when they have no symptoms, when they are physically inconspicuous, when average values are confirmed by testing blood and excreta which are also shown to contain no bacterial infestations, and when they appear to be reasonably fit. But actually not even 5 per cent of the population can be regarded as healthy when these criteria are met.

Seen esoterically, human beings are healthy when there is balance in the way their etheric and astral forces work together harmoniously and when the principles of their being are undisturbed by external influences and guided and developed in accordance with evolution by their spiritual centre, the 'I'.

Conversely, people are sick when they are dissatisfied with themselves and their surroundings, when they have a degree of pain, when their physical or mental fitness is impaired or when some function is not in order. They are not in balance psychologically and the principles of their being no longer work together as they should.

Individuals who have a 'supernatural' ability to sense the seat of an illness or a disposition towards a disease generally encounter much scepticism. We are used to illnesses being visible and open to diagnosis; we think they can only be treated medically by a trained practitioner. And everything is done to promote this view. There are, however, some signs of new thinking in Anglo-Saxon countries. People with these unusual abilities are able to sense changes in how the various principles of the human being work together, or they see alterations in the colours of a person's aura even before a disease becomes physically evident.

It can take a long time, sometimes many years, before pathological changes in the collaboration of the four principles of the human being show up as a physical illness. This is because the physical body is the oldest and most perfect of these principles and therefore the best able to resist pathogenic influences and other effects resulting in structural changes. One example of this is the length of time a heart can withstand countless instances of damage inflicted on it by our way of life (e.g. the use of nicotine, other detrimental chemical substances or also stress) before it becomes ill.

Although the physical body is more stable and mature in its structure than are the other three principles, nevertheless it is these latter that direct and influence how it is built up and maintained.

As a summary of all esoteric Mystery wisdom, spiritual science tells us that at a specific point in the evolution of our solar system certain retarded beings from the Old Moon stage influenced the overall conception of how the human being would be structured. These luciferic beings and their helpers interfered in human astrality in ways that ran counter to proper evolution even before the 'I' could become fully incorporated and begin to work. Such influences remain in subsequent ages, and even today they result in many consequences along the path of human evolution.

The personality that had as yet not come fully under the control of the 'I' succumbed to such tendencies and influences. It became more susceptible to desires and also more egoistic. In consequence moral awareness declined which made it possible for ahrimanic forces to have an effect at the etheric level.

Ahriman has taken possession of intellectuality in a way that has destroyed its connection with heart, soul and morality. Those who adapt to this develop a loveless way of looking at their environment. The luciferic influence leads to effusiveness, passionate excesses, exaggerated fancies and every form of affectation, whereas Ahriman enters into the human being more with falsehoods and excessively technical ideas.

When people succumb to these influences the consequences initially remain imperceptible and are more or less consciously fixed only in the life of soul. But when the individual has passed through the portal of death and experienced the period of kamaloca, all the consequences of his actions and ideas imbue the organizing principle that will build up the formative forces for that human being's next incarnation.

In this way ahrimanic influences become the cause of diseases that later work in the ether body, while luciferic consequences usually manifest in the formative concepts of the astral body, and later—in subsequent incarnations—also in the ether body.

This is the point: the human being is not a solitary, isolated being in the cosmos. He re-encounters everything during his sojourn in the spiritual world between death and a new birth. On the way down to a new incarnation he draws on the substrates of earlier actions and behaviour when putting together the principles of his being.

In the lower spiritual world actions are registered which, under the leadership of the spirits working there, bring it about that in his next life a person is guided to specific locations and confronted with certain external destiny events. If he acquired abundant intellectual and moral understanding, if his deeds were for the most part free of egoism, and if he made good, meaningful use of his life, then he will have a strong and stable constitution that is able to withstand diseases. Drives and passions, on the other hand, show up in the next life as a disposition to organic weakness.

Rudolf Steiner gave the recommendation: 'By strengthening our spirit of humility and modesty we protect ourselves against Lucifer. Contentedness with our destiny coupled with knowledge prevents Ahriman from taking effect.'

As they developed in the time of Old Sun, human beings possessed only the physical and ether bodies with an awareness that was even more unconscious than deep sleep is today. The astral body developed during the time of Old Moon and with it the possibility of feeling pain.

If the balance between ether and physical body is upset to a degree in which the etheric principle works too strongly on the physical without there being any involvement of the astral body, no pain is felt. This is why diseases emanating from the ether body are painless, which means they are more dangerous and pernicious.

There are levels of consciousness in the human being that are so profound as to be imperceptible even to the 'I'. This can result in diseases arising which are needed for a person's karma. Knowing reflection or wise forethought notwithstanding, situations can arise which are not recognized by normal consciousness for what they are, and this can lead to actions or accidents that appear to be entirely incomprehensible.

Everything in a person's behaviour that smacks of desire, selfishness, ambition, pride or vanity, all characteristics that tend towards asserting one's own ideas or personal opinions are always to a greater or lesser degree the consequence of luciferic influences in the astral body. If such attitudes are pursued in spite of this, the consequences, depending on the prevailing circumstances and their effects, become karmic tendencies that determine one's future destiny while it is being prepared between death and a new birth. In a new life the outcome may well be an incarnation in which one is disposed towards illness. If such an illness is overcome through spiritual development, greater confidence and stronger morality ensue which can later combat subsequent similar attacks.

To enable such disorders to be recognized for what they are, luciferic illnesses are accompanied by pain. So pain must be regarded as a warning to change one's lifestyle in order to avoid the causes of disease.

Wherever there is pain, this is a sign that luciferic forces have led to the illness. However, it cannot be concluded that all painful illnesses are exclusively caused by luciferic tendencies, for there may also be varying degrees of influence coming from ahrimanic forces. These involve the etheric rather than the astral level and therefore the symptoms are less painful.

Lucifer can also enable ahrimanic forces to work in more from the surroundings. This leads to fundamental changes in the way ether body and physical body collaborate, initially without any involvement on the part of the astral body. The changes come about at the deeply unconscious level below the pain threshold. Since pain is not a symptom, the pathological changes in the organism are much more pernicious.

If luciferic influences are the cause of the disease, the warning signals given by the helping powers involve pain. In other cases the function of an organ can be so reduced as to lead to paralysis. If balance is not restored, death ensues. But this can still have beneficial consequences, for in the next incarnation the organ in question will be vitally healthy and resistant to disease.

This brings us to an important law of karma that provides an explanation for further questions. When death is caused by an incurably diseased organ, the same organ will be especially healthy and strong in the next incarnation. The powers of opposition are only interested in taking possession of the human being at the level of the three lower principles of his being but not in causing his destruction and death. So death as a consequence of disease cannot be ascribed to their activity but should be seen as assistance rendered by powers working in accordance with creation.

Knowledge about reincarnation and karma was so much taken for granted in former times that it scarcely required any special mention. But now the time has come for a change and renewal of culture to be brought about through once more becoming aware of these things. Questions about the meaning and course of life can only be answered by knowledge about reincarnation and karma. This is what throws light on good fortune and misfortune, on sickness and health.